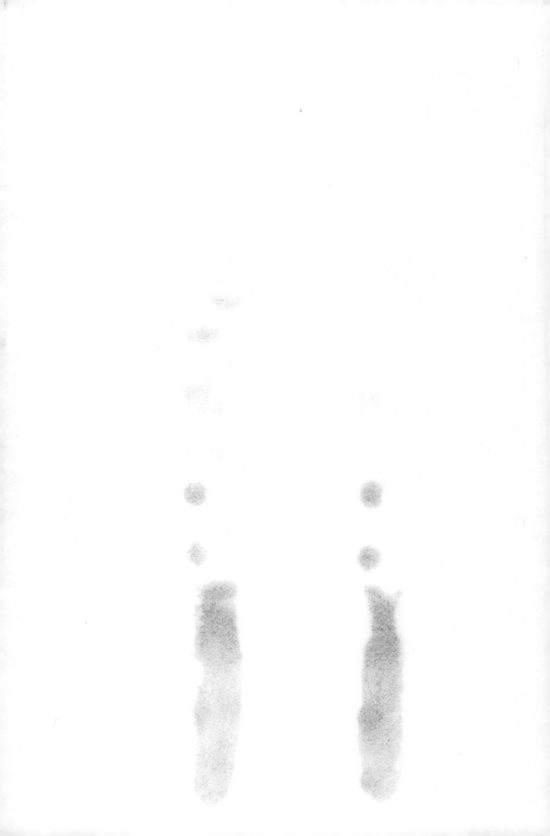

LETTER

PERFECT

HOW TO WRITE
BUSINESS LETTERS THAT WORK

LETTER PERFECT

HOW TO WRITE
BUSINESS LETTERS THAT WORK

Ferd Nauheim
Direct Mail and Marketing Consultant

VNR VAN NOSTRAND REINHOLD COMPANY
NEW YORK   CINCINNATI   TORONTO   LONDON   MELBOURNE

Copyright © 1982 by Van Nostrand Reinhold Company

Library of Congress Catalog Card Number: 81-14835
ISBN: 0-442-88021-9

Manufactured in the United States of America

Published by Van Nostrand Reinhold Company
135 West 50th Street, New York, N.Y. 10020

Van Nostrand Reinhold Limited
1410 Birchmount Road
Scarborough, Ontario M1P 2E7, Canada

Van Nostrand Reinhold Australia Pty. Ltd.
17 Queen Street
Mitcham, Victoria 3132, Australia

Van Nostrand Reinhold Company Limited
Molly Millars Lane
Wokingham, Berkshire, England

15 14 13 12 11 10 9 8 7 6 5 4 3 2 1

Library of Congress Cataloging in Publication Data

Nauheim, Ferd.
    Letter perfect.

    Includes index.
    1. Commercial correspondence. I. Title.
HF5721.N39   1981b   808'.066651021   81-14835
ISBN 0-442-88021-9   AACR2

to James R. Dimond
a letter perfect friend and writer

CONTENTS

end with well-lubricated couplings. If there is need to cover more than a single subject in a letter, don't let the fresh thoughts become detours. Tie all of the points you cover together. If there is one subject of particular importance, bring it back into sharp focus at the end.

It is so easy to grant a request or to make an adjustment that you may fail to capitalize on a positive situation. Saying "Yes," may cost, but the cost can pay dividends if it is said in the right way. Say, "Yes" quickly. Put it up front, and then embellish on it. Give more than is expected. Cater to the reader's interests. You can gain a great deal when you do something a customer wants. Show your appreciation for the opportunity.

Before you write a letter of refusal give the request a lot of thought. Most people are ill at ease about asking for something, unless they feel the request is fully deserved. Given enough thought you may decide to bow to the wish. If you cannot do so, save face for the writer. Make it clear that the request was given genuine thought. Explain the refusal, if at all possible, from his or her viewpoint. Make your letter a sandwich; something pleasant on top, a meaty filling of the reasons for the negative response, end with a final layer of something positive.

Enthusiasm is catching. The most welcome personal sales people are enthusiasts. A letter cannot compete with a flesh and blood personable salesperson so it must make a strong effort to compensate. Look for it and you always can find a sincere reason to express yourself with enthusiasm. Even a letter replying to a bitterly expressed complaint can be bright and cheerful.

Where confidence is lacking there is little chance of getting whatever action you ask for. The surest way to win confidence is to guard against exaggeration, statements and claims that defy belief—even if they are factual. A letter cannot answer a reader's reactions and challenges, making it imperative that you avoid any statements that may be misunderstood.

will call, completing the sale by mail. Each calls for different techniques.

when a prospective customer has not bought provides the
opportunity to offer a series of viewpoints, sales points,
reasons why.

INTRODUCTION
HOW TO CAPTURE THE RIGHT
ATTITUDE IN YOUR LETTERS

Driving home from work one day I had my radio turned on. I happened to catch a health lecturer in the middle of his talk. He was selling some kind of vitamin capsules. The man was terrific. He was so darn good I made a point of turning him off just before he gave the final pitch naming the product. I was afraid I'd be tempted to buy.

His whole case was built on the lack of thought we usually give to the food and liquids we consume. He talked about the farmers who study everything they can get their hands on that instruct them in the feeding of pigs. They follow the instructions and their pigs grow big, fat, sleek, and toothsome. But the same people stuff themselves with dubios hot dogs, uncertain whiskey, cheap candy, and anything else that happens to come along.

The dollars they get for their pigs are more important than their own good health and longevity.

"Nutritionists," the pitchman said, "can give you a very accurate chemical analysis of the human body. They have studied and experimented. They know. They can tell you just how much you should eat of various types of food to discourage illness and to give your body strength and vigor."

Listening to him convinced me that there was a lot of truth in this pitch. What a shame, I thought, that letter writers can't turn for help to the counterpart of nutritionists.

I've never heard of any method of analyzing the attitudes present in a business letter writer's mind at a given moment. I don't know any way to prepare a chart showing prescribed percentages of interest, knowledge, tact, desire to help, skill with expression, and salesmanship. And if a way is found to make such an analysis, the genius who discovers it will have to go further. He or she will have to find ways to create the ideal percentages to be applied when one faces the task of writing a particular kind of a letter.

Wouldn't it be wonderful if you could pick up a capsule labeled, "take immediately before writing an answer to a complaint." You'd swallow the capsule, and up would pop the perfect balance of mental attitude.

But there is no Santa Claus...no Easter Bunny...no Attitude Capsule.

You have to create the proper balance of attitudes the hard way. You have to create it, and you have to learn how to hold it until the task at hand is completed.

This book devotes itself to the mental attitudes that can produce letters that ring with sincerity, clarity, and warmth. In these pages you'll find nothing about the proper forms of address, punctuation, grammar, or other technical aspects of business letter writing.

This book has a single mission. It attempts to help you to write letters that make the readers feel good about you and the firm you represent. That's all.

Business letters are written to people. Companies can't read. Presidents, regional managers, salespeople, editors, and customers are merely lables hiding people. Business, at any level, responds to human emotions, for business *is* people.

There are those who feel that a business letter should convey facts in a pure, cold vacuum. The people who read your letters are not pure, cold vacuums. The hardest bitten professional purchasing agents will favor the sellers capable of demonstrating interest in them and their problems. They will lean toward sellers who try to be pleasantly helpful, cooperative, considerate, and grateful. And whether the selling is done in person, or by words on paper, it doesn't matter.

Every business letter you write is a selling letter. A letter of response to a supplier who has offered you merchandise should sell. You want the best goods or service at the most favorable terms, and you want prompt attention. A letter refusing credit should sell. The applicant may be a good credit risk some day. He or she may buy for cash now.

Every letter you write does either of two things: it makes the reader think more of you and your company, or it makes the reader think less of you and your company.

You are going to see dozens of letters used by big businesses, by middle-size businesses and by minibusinesses. These are letters in use. They work. They give the writers and their companies the desired results.

But there are no absolutes about effective business letter writing. Businesses (the people who speak for them) and the people they speak to are too dissimiliar. Good business letter writing should be as free and as flexible as good coversation: for that is what it is: coversation on paper.

While there are some important guidelines there are no strict rules of procedure. For example, no one can state that certain types of letters must consist of thus-and-so number of words or pages. A fishing captain I know keeps a group of customers loyal to him thanks, to a great extent, to a two-word postcard he uses at appropriate times: "They're running!" And you will read a single page letter that resulted in a $350,000 sales. But Chapter 5 will point out that when you have to write a letter of refusal, it just might pay to make it a multipage letter.

Speaking of long letters, there is a mistaken notion that a business letter that wanders off the rigid, frigid path of conveying pure information becomes a long letter. It's not necessarily so.

Dear Mr. Breyer

This is to acknowledge your favored order of June 17th for 7 gross of Shatterproof Bubble Gum No. 5. Shipment will be made on or about the end of the month.

Very truly yours,

or

Dear Mr. Breyer,

My heartiest thanks for the June 17th order. I'll see to it that the 7 gross of Shatterproof Bubble Gum No. 5 will be shipped before the month ends.

Cordially,

Both letters contain all the facts. The second letter, however, has a giant measure of an added ingredient. It is four words shorter, and it goes much further.

The real difference between weak and strong letters is attitude. The first letter writer had the attitude that it was his or her job to write letters confirming orders. The second letter writer had the attitude that it was his or her job to write letters confirming orders, being gracious to customers, imparting the feeling that the company will take a personal interest in the proper handling and prompt shipping of the order, and that the folks in his or her company are nice people to do business with.

As you read, and you begin to create new mental attitudes when you write letters, you will find you have gained somthing extra for yourself. You will find that writing business letters can be as enjoyable and as stimulating as having a spirited, happy chat with a good friend. And when that day comes you will know you are writing mighty good business letters.

Ferd

Look at that. The fellow who wrote this book signs the introduction with his first name. Never saw that before—but it is friendly.

FIRST PICTURE
THE PEOPLE
YOU ARE WRITING TO

A letter is supposed to give somebody information. That's why it is written. It's almost impossible to write a letter that fails to convey some information. A child can do that much, but when you give a letter added duties and qualities, do you become creative?

A GOOD BUSINESS LETTER WRITER MUST BE CREATIVE

Your letters may be designed to win new customers, to keep old customers, to accept or refuse credit, to handle adjustments, or to win the cooperation of suppliers. In any of those letters you are trying to accomplish something. You are trying to create a good feeling about your organization and that creates something else: a problem.

You are selling. Let's face it, no matter what kind of letters you write, if you aim to make people feel that your organization is a fine one, which deserves their high regard, you are selling.

If you have taken courses in salesmanship or have read books and articles on the subject, one of the first things you have learned was that star salespeople have one thing in common. Before they call on new prospects, they do some digging. They learn all they can about these propects: their names, occupations, income ranges, hobbies, likes and dislikes, and lots more.

Your language must be the reader's language. Armed with all the facts they can gather, professional salespeople approach prospects with confidence. They can talk the prospects' language. Once they come face to face with their potential customers they quickly pick up additional advantages. They see what their prospects look like and absorb the physical surroundings. They size up each individual's personality, disposition, present mood, and how employees and associates act in their presence. All these observations are valuable trail marks. The alert salesperson follows that trail to reach each prospect's interest. It is a short-cut to winning confidence. These facts and observations are vital to successful selling.

Certainly no salesperson worthy of their title would talk in identical terms to a farmer and to a bank president. A superior salesperson wouldn't talk in the same terms to a bank president and to a vice-president.

ALL LETTER WRITERS ARE SALESPEOPLE

Regardless of the purpose of your letters, you are a salesperson. You have to school yourself to do all the things other salespeople have found to be essential to success. There's one difference. No letter can do as thorough a selling job as a flesh and blood individual engaged in face-to-face selling. For that reason, when selling by letter, you have to be even more painstaking, and thoughtful. You have to compensate for the disadvantages.

Stop Answering Letters and Start Answering People

The mind is a delicate instrument. It will travel in any direction with just a gentle prod. Your mind follows brain boulevards you have established through habit. To change the direction, you must change some habits. Most businesspeople habitually think, "I must answer this letter."

At the office you think, "I must answer this letter," but if you get a letter at home—a letter from a friend—you say, "I have to answer Bill."

There is a world of difference in the way the two letters are written. When the signal to the letter writing department on your mind is, "Answer this letter," you do just that. You write to a piece of paper with markings on it. When the control room says, "Write to Bill," the letter you write is a warm, human document, full of personality, catering to Bill's viewpoint.

Bill gets pleasure and satisfaction from the letter he receives. The originator of the *letter* you answer gets cold, colorless information.

Form a new habit. Say, think, and feel, "Let's answer Bill." Stop saying and thinking, "Let's answer this letter."

Know whom you're writing to. That's not easy. Some of your letters may be to people you know, and that is fine. A great number of your letters, however, are written to people you've never met. You can't be the direct salesperson checking up on the person involved. Chances are that the letter writer you are responding to is far away, unknown to anyone in your office—just a name and a number on a letterhead or a ledger card—an unknown who wrote a letter of inquiry.

What you do know is that you are addressing an individual, filled with all the hopes, the doubts, the fears, the human attributes, the failings, and the prejudices you'll find in all individuals. But with each individual the quantities vary. That's what makes them individuals.

A LETTER IS A VERY PERSONAL DOCUMENT

Over the years I've acquired a lot of friends. At Christmas time, each year, I hear from a number of them. And because, in many cases, it is the only time of the year that we correspond, most of those cards have something more than the standard holiday greetings. There are a few handwritten lines bringing me up to date on what they are doing, how many children they have, and so on. It's up to me to write to each of them and tell them what my pesonal status is these days. Last year I heard from seven such miles-away friends.

When I replied I had the same information to give to each of them but I found it necessary to write seven entirely different letters. I know these people. I know how they differ. A uniform letter may have been fine for one of them but it would have been all wrong for the other six.

The uniform letter would have made Dick feel I was getting mightly shallow. It would have made Martha think I was bragging. It would have made Herb think I'd lost my sense of humor. It would have made Lowell think I'd become stuffy, and so on.

When you stop to think about that in terms of the letters you write to people unknown to you, it's frightening, isn't it? Only one out of seven would have been right. You can't afford to write business letters that have so low a batting average. *What can you do to compensate for the fact that you haven't met and haven't heard anything about the people you write to?*

HOW TO BE A LETTER DETECTIVE

You probably have read detective stories from time to time. If you have, you've come across cases where a letter from an unknown party turns up. The crime-detecting technicians analyze the paper and the ink. A handwriting analyst makes a study. The detective hero, who generally is a psychologist and a collector of rare false teeth, makes deductions.

By the time all the reports are assembled they could recognize the writer on a dark night, lying face down in a pitch black alley. They know where he came from, what he does for a living, and when he had his appendectomy.

I'm not suggesting that you set up the counterpart of a crime-detection laboratory. I do suggest that you do a limited amount of detecting.

All inquiries tell you something about the writer. Any letter you receive—even a filled-in coupon from a magazine ad—can tell you something about the writer. The part of the country it comes from tells you a lot: big city or small town. The envelope, the stationery, the handwriting or typing, the manner of expression, the spelling and punctuation, even the name tells stories. What is said, how it's expressed, the question asked, the method of payment, are all parts of a big jigsaw puzzle. Your job is to put it together.

Letter detecting is not time consuming. It sounds like a long, slow task, but it isn't at all. True, you'll take some extra time when you first tackle this fascinating job. But if you give it your full attention for a few days, you'll soon find yourself doing it automatically. As you pick up a letter, certain features will jump at you. It will become automatic for you to absorb the tell-tale marks at a glance. In a matter of seconds you'll have some knowledge of the writer.

You won't always be right. In some cases a further exchange of letters will give you an entirely new picture of the writer. In some cases you'll never find out you were wrong. But you will hit the bull's eye in many instances. You will be right, and you'll be writing far more effective letters in *most* cases.

As you perfect yourself as a letter detective you'll be pleasantly businesslike with Betty Blowe and folksy with Oscar Zilch. You'll spell it out for John Jones and summarize for Helen White. You'll see the need for flattering Tom Green and for laughing with Harry Johnson.

THE GREATEST SECRET OF ALL: TRANSPOSE

And here's the greatest secret of all in this whole subject of writing the right kinds of letters to the right kinds of people. Once you've made your analysis and determined the kind of a person your correspondent is, *transpose*! You've met thousands of individuals. Some made vivid impressions on you. They're with you in your memory always—very alive and very real. They represent many types.

When you read fiction, consciously or subconsciously, you associate the characters in the story with people you've known. They become real flesh and blood individuals to you. If I say, "Bookworm," you get a mental image of a bookworm you know pretty well. If I say, "Flaky," up comes another picture of somebody you know. It would be difficult for me to think of a descriptive term that would fail to produce some image for you.

That same reaction will take place once you've put a label on the person who wrote the letter you're answering. But that isn't enough. It isn't strong enough. Let the old friend you remember *become* the person who is to get a letter from you.

Write to a friend. The mental picture you have formed of a woman who wrote to you makes you think of your friend Hattie. Sharpen your memory of old Hattie and mentally start your letter, "Dear Hattie." Keep Hattie in there working for you. Talk to Hattie all through the letter. She's somebody you really know. You understand a great deal about Hattie. You'll be talking her language. Your letter will come to life. After you have composed your "Dear Hattie" letter you may have to eliminate a phrase here and a sentence there, but your final letter will radiate warmth.

AMERICAN AIRLINES WRITES TO A "FRIEND"

Here's a letter received by the Washington office of American Airlines.

> Gentlemen:
>
> I'm 82 years old. I've never flown in a plane and always promised myself that maybe some day I would. My boy Harry will be 50 this coming July 8th and since he lives down in Dallas now I thought maybe this is the time to keep that promise to myself.
>
> Now I will tell you frankly a man my age gets nervous thinking about things like flying way up in the air and I hear you have to be strapped

down the whole time and another thing, I do not think I like the idea of nothing but cold things to eat and I can't see how you can safely cook in an airplane.

You send me the rates and let me know how long it takes and if you have anything to say about those other things I would like to know about them.

Respectfully,

Martin Grimes

Can you picture Martin Grimes? Our mental images of him may vary some, but let's take his handwritten letter and see what kind of a portrait we can draw. No youngster, of course. I see him as a spare man with a few strands of pure white hair. There's a bit of a twinkle in his eye and a good crop of well-embedded smile wrinkles in his face. He's sentimental. He likes to talk. There's a good measure of the sport left over from his younger days. He likes life and likes people. He realizes that, at his age, he should take care of himself and feels just a little foolish about taking his first flight at 82. He's hoping that all of his fears and doubts will be wiped out by the answer he gets from the airline. He's mighty anxious to fly.

This answer is in step with the reader

Dear Mr. Grimes,

I envy you, Mr. Grimes. There's nothing I can think of quite as wonderful as a first flight. And this will be a first flight in one of American's 727 luxury jets. I'm excited about it myself. The things I'm going to tell you make me feel that I'm the one bringing you and your son together for this fine occasion.

You have no reason to worry about flying way up in the air. The 727, like all of our modern jets, is fully pressurized. You'll feel as comfortable and secure as if you were seated in your favorite chair in your own home. And you can forget about being strapped down. For a few minutes when the plane takes off and again when it lands your flight attendant will ask you to fasten your seat belt. During the rest of the flight you can get up, move around, do whatever you want.

And here's another happy surprise. You'll be served a fine hot lunch while in flight. This is possible because of the specially designed ovens that have been developed for heating or cooking meals in flight in a matter of minutes. Hot coffee, cold milk, and soft drinks are yours for the asking at any time.

The flight you would find most enjoyable leaves Washington's Dulles

International Airport at 7:45 on the morning of July 8th. Three hours and fifteen minutes later, which is 10 a.m. Texas time, you'll be in the Dallas – Fort Worth area saying, "Happy Birthday," to your son. The round-trip fare is $358, which includes all taxes, and you'll enjoy it while in the air.

Here's what I've done. I have reserved a seat for you on that airplane. If you will call me, at your convenience, I will take care of the details of the return flight and will make arrangements to hold your tickets for pick-up, or I'll mail them to you at your home as part of our tickets-by-mail program. When we talk, I will tell you how to arrange for limousine service to the airport. My phone number is 857-4210.

And when you see your son in Dallas, Mr. Grimes, please give him my warm wishes for a happy birthday too.

Cordially,

Michael F. Buckley
Manager of Passenger Sales—
Washington
AMERICAN AIRLINES

Mr. Buckley is a fine salesman. He has a feeling for people. When he wrote to Mr. Grimes he could visualize the man. The attitude he adoped created a letter that blended with his mental image of his potential passenger. Had he been face to face with Mr. Grimes he would have used the same language he put on paper.

Answering a cold, formal letter. There will be times when the letter you receive is cold and formal. The writer of any letter is a human being even though the manner some people adopt when writing business letters fails to reveal human qualities. Far too many charming individuals have the unfortunate notion that business correspondence should be devoid of warmth and color.

When replying to such letter writers you can't afford to gamble on being as free and friendly as Mr. Buckley was in his letter. If you want your reply to be rich with personality and the suggestion that your company must have good people to deal with, however, you will avoid the temptation to follow the style of a stiff and formal writer.

A COLD LETTER AND A WARM REPLY

Robert Cadel, publisher of Urban Design Newsletter, received this letter.

Dear Mr. Cadel,

This is to acknowledge receipt of your form letter of recent date soliciting my subscription to your Urban Design Newsletter. I have heard of your publication on numerous occasions but have never seen a copy. The facts that have come to my attention and the literature forwarded to me by your office lead me to surmise that the issues may bring to my attention timely news regarding my profession.

In consideration of the fact that I am immensely busy and the nature of my work requires an exceptional amount of reading I am reluctant to burden myself with additional matter. If, therefore, your publication is not in excess of a single lettersize sheet this is your authorization to enter our subscription for a one year term.

Very truly yours,

J.M.L _____

The letter; from a well known architectural firm, was signed by the president. Mr. Cadel's newsletter averages about twelve pages. This was his reply.

Dear Mr. L _____

When a busy man like you takes time out to express his interest in Urban Design Newsletter I am deeply gratified. Thank you, Mr. L _____.

In your letter you have summarized the very reason why the Newsletter was created. It was brought into existence because leaders in the urban design field are immensely busy—because the day-to-day requirement of keeping themselves fully informed demands a vast amount of reading and research.

Urban Design Newsletter is not additional reading matter. The editors do a good deal of your reading for you. They take long articles and reports and condense them to a few brief sentences—sentences that give you the facts you want and need. Add to this the frequent reports of significance originated by the staff.

The Newsletter reports on every facet of urban design. The areas it covers require more than a single letter size page, but the parts you will select for reading will average a page or two per issue. As you will see when you examine the sample copy I'm giving you with this letter, each issue displays a highly condensed index of the contents at the top of page one. At a glance you'll see which articles you will want to read. The balance of the issue will make no demands on your time.

There is no need for you to take the time to reply to this letter, Mr.

L _____. Because Urban Design Newsletter will enable you to cut down on your reading time, and because you will not have more than a page or two of important facts to read, I'm taking the liberty of entering your annual subscription unless I hear from you to the contrary.

My warmest thanks.

Sincerely,

Robert Cadel

Trade on the writer's likes and dislikes. That's exactly what Mr. Cadel did in his letter of reply. Mr. L _____ had concealed his personality behind an iron curtain of flutter-butter, old-fashioned language. But he gave publisher Cadel a break. He told him what he likes and doesn't like. In his reply Mr. Cadel was a personable human being. In clear, compelling terms he stated why his publication would give Mr. L _____ just what he wanted.

During one of its annual fund raising drives, the District of Columbia Lung Association received this letter from a prominent business man.

The "strictly business" approach

Dear Mrs. Paoletti:

In this morning's mail I received your appeal for a contribution to this year's campaign. Your letter suggests that my firm increase its customary contribution.

As a businessman, as you can appreciate, I am called upon to contribute to every campaign that comes down the pike. While we try to play an active role in community activities and to distribute funds allocated for charitable purposes judiciously, the demands are greater than the means.

In light of the well publicized advances that have been made in the conquering of TB I fail to see any justification for an increased donation. It is well known that TB is no longer the killer it once was, now that it can be successfully treated with drugs. In light of this I feel we are justified in reducing, rather than increasing, the sum to be given to your campaign.

If I am mistaken in my conclusions I shall be glad to review your counter claims.

Respectfully,

J.D.B._____

Mrs. Paoletti replied:

Dear Mr. B_____,

Your November 17th letter was most welcome, for it reaffirms once again the fact that members of our local business establishment are keenly aware of, and concerned about, the needs of our community. While your present views may cause you to question our appeal for increased funds, I know that you will give this reply thoughtful consideration.

Your impressions about TB are accurate. The onetime "white plague" has been dealt a telling blow by advances made possible through research. Drugs and improved treatment techniques have dramatically reduced not only the death rate, but the number of people who contract TB. This is true on a nationwide basis.

The shameful reality, however is that our city still has one of the highest incidences of TB in the nation. Lulled by a false sense of security when the dramatic results of the new drugs became apparent, government funds for TB control were drastically cut about 10 years ago. One has only to look at statistical charts since then to see that the action was a mistake. Compared to the declining TB rates enjoyed by other cities, we remain on a plateau. Even more troubling is the suspicion of many informed public health professionals that up to 50 percent of new cases never get reported, meaning that the situation is considerably more serious than the published figures indicate.

Our association has pledged itself to changing the shocking statistics. Armed with the knowledge that TB is preventable, treatable, and curable, we have mounted a concerted, aggressive campaign to have Federal and municipal funds restored to the TB control budget. We will not rest until our residents have available the modern TB control program to which they have a right.

We intend to achieve our goal despite political and bureaucratic complexities with which you, as a business man, are doubtless, familiar. We need your support, and hope your firm will see its way clear to increasing its financial contribution. We also invite you to help us in an equally important way. Join us as a volunteer, lending your time and talents to an activity that will benefit every resident of and visitor to our beautiful city.

My warmest thanks for giving me the opportunity to respond to your concerns, and to share ours with you.

Yours sincerely,

Theresa Paoletti
Executive Director

Mrs. Paoletti's letter reveals her proper mental picture of an astute, civic-minded businessman. Her letter is devoid of tugs at the heart strings. It is devoted entirely to the *business* viewpoint of the problem. The letter resulted in an increased contribution. Another charitable institution, the Columbia Lighthouse for the Blind was faced with the need to change the viewpoint of a contributor.

Let's look at one final example of a letter correcting a misunderstanding and reflecting the writer's mental picture of a person he has never met.

Whoever is in charge,

I recently sent a $25 contribution to the Columbia Lighthouse, but cross me off your list. Less than a month after I made the donation I had a letter from you with a make-believe bank book in it asking me to make a contribution. That didn't bother me, I figured that it was mailed with no one knowing that I had just given. Then I started getting letters asking me to return the book.

I did not keep your bank book so I can't return it, and even if I did have it I don't think I'd bother to send it back. Do take me off your list.

Mrs. Arthur L _____

Charles Fegan, Executive Director of the Columbia Lighthouse for the Blind, had no trouble picturing Mrs. L _____ and understanding the reasons why she expressed herself the way she did. This was his response:

Dear Mrs. L _____,

The best friends the Lighthouse has are those who have reason to be provoked with us and take the trouble to tell us so. Had you not written I would not have had this opportunity to explain, and to ask your forgiveness and understanding.

Mrs. L _____, we cherish donors as generous as you. There are not very many. That is why we must use mass mailings in order to realize the funds that are so vital to support the many services we render to the visually handicapped. Over the past two decades we have experimented with various mail appeals and never have found one that brings in as much money as the bank book appeal. And, because we do mail in large quantities it is economically impossible to check our lists against the records of gifts from such thoughtful givers as you. The cost would be prohibitive.

Experience has taught us that it is wasteful not to request the return of the little books. Not only do we save much printing expense by getting them back, but many good people, who had planned to give but had forgotten, are reminded of their good intentions. They enclose a donation when the book is mailed back to us.

I'm so glad you gave me the chance to tell our story, but, just in case I have failed to explain the problem as fully as I would like, I'm going to take the liberty of phoning you in the next day or two.

Cordially,

Charles Fegan,
Executive Director

The opening statement in Charles Fegan's letter invites reading. Here is a lady who says, "Take me off your list. I'll never give again," and, to her surprise the answer she receives starts out by saying she is one of the Columbia Lighthouse's best friends.

Mr. Fegan was able to see, in his mind's eye, what type of person Mrs. L _____ was. He pictured a good, generous woman—a little bit on the sensitive side—thoroughly angry when she wrote her letter. What better way to soften her grim anger than to start his reply with that expression of friendship? Having softened her attitude, he then was in a position to speak to an open mind, which he did, giving full and satisfying detail of the situation that had antagonized her.

MAIN CONSIDERATIONS WHEN PICTURING THE PEOPLE TO WHOM YOU WRITE

1. Start with the attitude that you must create confidence and a warm feeling about your company.

2. Keep in mind that you are selling and must think as a salesperson.

3. To influence people, a good salesperson must speak the reader's language.

4. To speak that language, you must stop answering letters and start answering people.

5. If you are to answer the people you are writing to in language they'll understand and appreciate, you must be a letter detective.

6. Form the habit of studying every inquiry for clues to the writer's nature and personality.

7. Transpose. Form a picture of the writer and then think of a friend with the same characteristics.

8. Write to your friend.

9. When answering a cold, formal letter, dig a little deeper till you find something that represents the writer or, at least, the writer's basic interests.

10. When the writer reveals anger, you must reduce or eliminate that attitude before giving your explanation.

2

GIVE YOUR LETTERS
A RUNNING START

Will my letter be read? As a writer of business letters you constantly face this question. You face an additional and more important question: Will my letter be read with full attention?

When responding to someone you may say, "Of course my letter will be read. I'm replying to an inquiry, or to a customer who uses our products or services, or this is a person who needs what we offer."

You are right—up to a point. When you write letters of reply, or to customers, or to thoroughly qualified prospects, you have reason to assume that the reader has genuine interest in what you have to say.

People are mentally lazy. All professional letter writers know that the average readers of their letters hate to do any unnecessary thinking. There are countless demands on readers' interests and attention. People need a jolt if you want them to think.

The mind of the average letter reader is like a balky mule. You have to build a fire under it to make it go. Maybe your letter isn't intended to encourage the reader to do something. Maybe it isn't even intended to convey information of any great importance. Still, you took the time and trouble to compose that letter for specific reasons. You, at the very least, want to plant a thought or convey an impression. You won't accomplish your purpose if you fail to make the reader read and think and, in most cases, act.

PUT THE READER'S MIND IN GEAR

Television, radio, newspapers, movies, books, magazines, and all forms of advertising have made all of us spectators. Our mental transmissions spend more time in neutral than in gear. If your letters are supposed merely to entertain or provide escape, you have very little to worry about. If they are intended to do more than that, you have to roll up your creative sleeves and work.

Television, radio, newspapers, movies, books, magazines, and advertisements have done you another disservice. They have accustomed the people you write to to being lured into watching, listening, or reading. They all use showmanship.

Put some bait on your hook. Look at the big, popular magazines; it doesn't matter which. Pick up any one of them. Just look at what the editors have done. You bought your copy of your "pet" magazine because you like the writers. You like the type of features and stories it carries.

Big money is paid to the authors because the editors know you like what they write. On top of that, they spend more big money to get a top illustrator. The artist creates additional lure and eye appeal. But the editors don't stop there.

They have found it necessary to throw a blurb (a bold type statement under each title) to induce you to read. You flip through the pages and you see a fictional story called, "The Schemer." Maybe you'll read it and maybe you won't. But right under the title it says, in big letters, "Did she know that the man she married was really her uncle?" Now your curiosity is hooked. Now you'll read.

Just think about that. If the editors of a magazine you have selected for yourself and have paid hard cash to get, know it's necessary to use such blurbs to make you read the kind of stories you *enjoy* reading, can you get away with less when you write a letter?

You can't.

THE OPENING WORDS CAN OPEN THE MIND

The opening statements in any sales talk—the first remarks made by a speaker, the first paragraph of a book, the first words of your letters— do either of two things. They tell the audience, "This is something I want to hear or read," or they say, "This sounds dull and unimportant. I can relax."

Well-trained sales people understand the rule. The salesperson in the drug store, trying to win a contest for selling the most shaving cream, opens with, "Would you like to cut your shaving time in half?"

The successful seller of a monthly sales training publication walks into a prospect's office and asks, "Would you be interested in hiring a highly successful sales manager for $12.50 a month?"

The door-to-door salesperson smiles and says, "Mrs. Thompson, your neighbor, asked me to see you."

The headlines on ads have the same mission. If the headline doesn't have eye appeal the rest of the ad is never read.

Make people want to read more. If testing and experience have proved that these various modes of communication need running starts, the same must be true of letters. Despite that, look at the depressing number of letters we get through the mail that start with such yawn producers as, "This is in reply to yours of January 17th." "We are writing to you to call your attention to a new service we are offering." And so on, *ad nauseam*.

How much more arresting it is to have the first example changed to read:

> "I'm going to do exactly what you asked in the letter
> you wrote on January 17th."

How much more enticing it is to switch the second letter opening to:

> "You're going to get enormous benefits from a new
> service that has just been made available to you."

No matter what the subject matter is, if you want people to read and you want alert attention, start off with a bang. Take a running start and have the reader running with you—not limping behind or running away from you.

WHERE TO START YOUR LETTER

Appreciating the importance of starting your letter with a crash of cymbals is one thing. Choosing the right thing to talk about is another. Examine the next dozen business letters you get. You'll find that a majority of them have one thing in common. They start slowly and then start running if they run at all.

Don't warm up on your letterhead. Most business letter writers, when they start dictating, typing, or penning a letter aren't totally sure of how they want to express themselves. Throughout the first paragraph they spin their wheels. They say unnecessary things. They fill that opening paragraph with weak and worn out expressions. They tell their readers things they already know. These fillers require no mental effort. While the writers' mouths or hands are busy, their minds are free to think about what they really want to say when they get to the meat of the matter.

Warming up mentally is fine, but don't do it on your letterhead. Think it through before you start the letter. Don't drag the reader with you while you are putting on your running shoes. Bring the reader into the act when you start to run.

Check back through the carbons of letters you have written. Just for fun, see how often your letters would have been far better and would have left out nothing vital *if you had just crossed out the first paragraph.*

Start with something the reader wants to know. That's always a safe bet. When you read the chapter on "How to Capitalize on a "Yes" you'll see many reasons why this pays.

An example of a warm, enticing opening. You've received a normal, humdrum letter from a good customer. Your customer says:

Dear So and So,

This is to advise you that we are opening a branch store on September first. Through an oversight we failed to place an order for a supply of your Model 2213R which we plan to include in our offering of opening specials. At this time I would like to order one (1) gross.

We are about to prepare our opening ads so please advise by return mail whether or not you can assure me of delivery in time for the opening.

Respectfully,

Janet Opener

A check with your production and shipping departments gives you the answer you want. You can deliver the merchandise on time. Here is your reply with an opening paragraph that is warm, informative, and immensely pleasing to Ms. Opener.

Dear Ms. Opener,

One gross of Model 2213R will attend the opening of your new branch store. The shipment is being rushed out of our warehouse this morning and with it goes our heartiest good wishes for great success in your new store.

With the shipment you'll find some point-of-purchase and window display material. These may prove valuable in dressing up for the big occasion and reminding folks of one of the many fine offerings you advertised.

If I can do anything else to help, please tell me. I'll be most interested to know how well your opening sale does. Here's hoping for an unqualified triumph.

Cordially,

Make a mental comparison with the cheerful, cooperative excitement in that opening paragraph and the heel-dragging conventional opening of the pompous business letter. Both letters convey facts, but this letter puts its arm around the buyer's shoulders and says, "Friend, I'm with you 100%."

Start with an intriguing question—Not just any question, but an intriguing one that ties directly to the main subject. A manufacturer of display racks for drug stores received an inquiry through the mail. His reply started with this question: "Would you pay an extra $5 a month rent if you could double the display space in your store?" A question like that, aimed directly at the reader's main interest, guarantees full attention to what follows.

Start with a shocking statement. "58 people in your community will die next week." Readers get a jolt from reading that. It makes them sit up and read with avid interest. Openings of this type must be handled with thoughtful care. They must be supported by what follows. If they fail to relate themselves to the heart of your message, leave them out. But an opening about 58 people dying next week can perform a real function for the insurance agent, the smoke detector distributor, and others who offer goods or services that can cut down on the forecast number of deaths or injuries.

Take a look at a letter with a shock opening, where the theme behind the shock statement follows through to the end.

Dear Mr. Renter,

You are paying entirely too much rent. Three days ago, on July 9th, you wrote to me and said that the only printing your bank needs is envelopes because you have your own printing and mailing department. After reading your letter I put on my hat and visited your bank.

What a busy, bustling successful bank you have!

I saw long lines of people at every teller's window. I saw people working on bookkeeping machines and on calculators in hallways. You are bursting at the seams. Then I went back to your printing and mailing shop. There I saw an area of at least 900 square feet devoted to my business, not to the banking business.

You need more space for banking operations. You have it. You are paying rent for it, but you aren't using it. That's why I contend that you are paying entirely too much rent.

If you closed out that printing and mailing section and turned all of that work over to my professional shop, the difference in your costs would be the cost of renting back to yourself that desperately needed 900 square feet. It would be the cheapest rent you ever paid. It would reduce your overall rent to a point where I no longer could say that you are paying too much.

I will phone you tomorrow for an appointment so that we can talk this over.

Sincerely,

You'll notice that the shock opening statement is never dropped. It is the heart and soul of the letter. It is not just a device to win original attention.

Start your letter with humor. (Chapter 15 is devoted to uses of humor throughout, not just as an opening attention winner.) People love to smile. They love to be entertained. A light touch of humor can sweep readers into your letters and carry them right down to your signature with unusual ease.

But be careful. Don't be funny just for the sake of being funny. It must be appropriate humor. It must be in excellent taste. It must never be the type of humor that could possibly offend. It must not be forced humor. If it isn't part and parcel of your basic message throw it out.

"Tomorrow morning at sunrise I am to be boiled in oil." That is the type of humor you can use with safety when writing to a customer who has inquired about a not too important error in a shipment. Don't use humor if the error was a serious one and the customer is red hot. The injured party doesn't think the situation is funny.

As an example of how humor *may* be used, suppose you manufacture a cosmetic item. One morning you receive a letter from a druggist who handles your line. The druggist tells you that your product is fine and the customers seem to like it, but the price is too high. It is suggested that you spend less on the fancy package and reduce the price.

This is your reply:

Dear Mr. Prescription,

I just finished reading your November 5th letter and I thought of the girl in the cotton stockings. You know what happened to the girl in the cotton stockings, don't you? Nothing.

The thought behind your suggestion is sound. If we could reduce the high cost of packaging we could sell for less and so could you. But we have learned, through testing, that when we fail to put sheer hosiery on our girl nobody wants to take her out.

Many of the items you handle can dress up in work clothes without injuring their popularity. Our little lady, however, is not of the working class. She's purely social. She could wear cotton stockings and have a heart of gold beneath them—though I'll confess those would be mighty high stockings—but nobody would ever know. She must have expensive glitter and charm if your customers are going to come courting.

Research has shown that smartly attired costmetics will give you rapid turnover even though the price reflects the high cost of the eye-appealing package. Just for an experiment put our product on the counter, right next to the cash register where her lovely legs will show, and see what a fine gold-digger she can be for you.

My deepest thanks for your thoughtful suggestion.

Cordially,

As in the case of the shock letter, the humor carries the entire message. In this case it was used to sell a point of view and it served a second important role, it eased the problem of turning down a customer's suggestion.

Start by writing the last paragraph first. When you read the chapter, "How to Put an Action Close in Your Letters," you'll see how this technique can be a great help if you have the problem of how to start.

If your last paragraph fulfills its true function it tells the reader exactly what to do or exactly what you will do. Many seasoned business letter writers have found that writing the last paragraph first gives the entire letter direction. When you start a letter, you are aiming at an objective. The straighter your aim the more likely you are to hit the target. When you write the last paragraph first you are setting up the target. With the target in sight the first paragraph becomes far easier to compose.

GETTING INSTANT AND FULL ATTENTION WITH UNPERSONALIZED LETTERS

Mailings sent to fairly large numbers of people can get off to a running start even though the recipient is not addressed by name. Actually, because the opening is the first thing seen, you can seize the reader's interest without delay. Here are a few examples of fast starts of that nature.

Lower your taxes now
and have more income
when you retire . . . .

> The Federal government offers you that dual benefit if you qualify, and I think you do. The reason why I believe . . . .

There's one way
to be sure that your
business gifts will
get a sincere
"Just what I wanted!"

> There's absolutely no need to gamble that the dollars you spend on seasonal business gifts may get cold, indifferent receptions. What you're about to read will tell you how you can give your customers the real pleasure of picking out what they want, without knowing the cost and without being at all embarrassed. You can picture . . . .

Sales contests can plague you
with a mountain of detail . . . or . . .
you can let us climb those
mountains for you.

> As specialists in planning highly profitable sales contests we've researched every problem that may arise and every pesky detail that must be foreseen. If you will look . . . .

A digger that can

dig 2 holes faster than

you can read this letter . . . .

> Thanks for asking for facts about our fence post hole digger. The speed, the rugged construction, the flexibility of . . . .

How you and your family

will live is about to change . . . .

> No matter what the outcome of the November elections, how you may live in the years ahead . . . even where you may live . . . can be changed. Whether the change will be great or small—good or bad—remains to be seen. But the more you know about the forces that can create those changes, the better fortified you can be to protect, or to capitalize. That is why . . . .

We asked 37 housewives to

use this new appliance for

just one week and then to

tell us what they thought.

Not one of them let us take it back!

> Just take a moment to look at the pictures and the story about this grand new time and space saver and you'll see why . . . .

Although each of the examples shown addresses itself to a different type of audience, and deals with a different type of product, they have one thing in common. Without exception, the writers of those attention demanding openings looked for and used *the biggest benefit each of the products offers*. Doesn't that make sense? If anything you have to say is calculated to make a potential buyer want more information, surely it is the most valuable aspect of whatever you are selling. No need to worry that everything else you have to say will diminish in importance. You can and should come full circle. You'll approach the close of your letter by restating the major sales point.

THE DATE AND FILE NUMBER OF THE SENDER'S LETTER

Few things make a letter drag its feet as much as an opening sentence or paragraph that recites the date on the inquirer's letter and any other identifying information. Including such data in your letter leads to stuffy, antiquated openings such as, "This is in response to yours of September 17th, file number 226−O−A, Procurement and Specification Division." Even though the person reading your letter may know that you had to give that information, can't you just hear the snoring start?

Eliminate reference information where it isn't needed. Putting these dull, dry facts into a letter has become a tried and tired business practice. In many cases it is not needed at all. Mrs. Willowby writes to say she can't find a local dealer who sells your product. She wants to know how to get one. You don't have to give her facts that will enable her to search her files so that she'll know what she wrote to you. That's true of many small business firms too. You can tell from the nature of the letter, and from the source, whether or not they will recall writing to you when they receive your response. If logic tells you that identification of the sender's letter is not needed, *leave it out.*

When reference data are essential. There are two ways to handle it without letting it spoil your opening. If the date of the inquirer's letter is all that's needed, the problem is simple. Blend it into your first sentence. You don't have to say, "This is in response to your letter of September 16th." Obviously it is the response. There's no need to waste the reader's time or your own specifying what is known.

> "The 2 gross of Kill-Rats-Dead pellets you ordered on September 17th left here this morning."

> "When you inquired about the deluxe editions, on September 17th, I wonder whether you knew of the extra profit in this line?"

Once you accept the fact that there is no need to make a feature of the date on the sender's letter, you have licked this serious problem.

When it becomes necessary to go into greater detail. To identify the original letter of inquiry, you must resort to other measures. It no longer becomes easy and natural to blend it in. It sounds a bit silly to say, "When you inquired about the deluxe editions, on September 17th, file number 226−O−A, Procurement and Specifications Division, I wonder whether you knew of the extra profit in this line?" But when writing replies to inquiries from huge corporations, the Government, and other involved institutions, the need for such identification becomes a necessary evil. In such cases, remove it from the body of the letter. Set it off by itself at the very top of your letterhead, a few lines below the date.

LETTERHEAD

September 20th, 1980

RE: Your letter, September 17th, 1980
      File No. 226 – O – A
      Procurement and Specifications Division

Dear Ms. Holland,

Now you've removed the road block and all is clear sailing.

THINGS TO REMEMBER WHEN YOU START YOUR LETTER

1. Remember that people are mentally lazy.
2. You must lure them into reading with full attention.
3. Your first words set the reader's mental stage.
4. Start with a bang.
5. Warm up in your mind—not on your letterhead.
6. Tell readers something they want to know.
7. Use an intriguing question.
8. Make a shocking statement.
9. Start with humor.
10. Write the last paragraph first.
11. Don't use reference data where not needed.
12. Where they are needed, blend the date on the sender's letter into a compelling opening sentence.
13. Where a volume of reference data is needed, remove it from the body of your letter.
14. Open with the greatest benefit.

3

MAKE YOUR LETTERS
FLOW SMOOTHLY

Every letter you write has a variety of missions. Not the least of these is the assurance that the reader will actually read. There's a vast difference between reading and skimming. When your letter of reply to an inquiry is received, the one who gets it will look for the answer to his or her question. Chances are that you have answered the question and have put in some additional ingredients. You put them in for a purpose. If the reader merely skims your letter looking for your answer, your efforts have been wasted.

The beginning is just a beginning. You have seen what you must do with the very first words in your letter if you want to give the reader the feeling that the entire letter should be read with full attention. But there is no guarantee that it will be.

Abrupt shifts from one thought to another stop the reader. Each shift of thought can be a rock or a rut in the road. Your first paragraph may provide the requested information, as it should. You have that out of the way. Now you want to talk about a new product your company is introducing. If you fail to blend the two thoughts, you have required your readers to make an abrupt stop. When they stop, they may decide that it's a good place to get off. The readers have gotten the information they wanted. They're busy. They may put your letter aside.

Use smooth "connectors" to fill the ruts in the road. Short paragraphs are excellent in letters. They give the impression, even though the letter may be lengthy, that it is an easy, quick letter to read.

Each time you start a new paragraph, however, you may be providing a stopping-off point. The first words of each paragraph should be "connectors." The first words should link the new paragraph to the former one for smooth reading, devoid of stops and starts.

When you start a paragraph with words such as "But," "And," "That's why," and the like, you have smoothed out the road. The use of some of these words at the start of a sentence may offend the strict grammarian. I apologize to the grammarians. But, as business letter writers, we are more interested in effectiveness than in the rules of grammar.

LINKING A SERIES OF THOUGHTS TOGETHER

Here is a letter from one of the great department stores in Los Angeles. A woman mailed them a postcard asking whether a certain ad she recalled having seen was that store's ad. The writer wanted to tell her she was right, wanted to call her attention to some services they offered, and wanted to invite her to open a charge account. This was the letter the customer received.

Dear Mrs. Blue,

You are right. The ad you recall about a special purchase of drapery fabrics was ours. Although many people hurried to our two stores in response to the ad, we still have these lovely materials and you will find a broad selection at the advertised prices.

And since you are thinking of new drapes for your home, Mrs. Blue, you'll be interested in the services offered by our Home Decorating Department. At your request one of our skilled decorators will visit your home. He or she will be happy to work with you and will offer suggestions as to types of materials, color combinations, and the most effective methods of hanging your drapes. There is no charge for this. You'll find that our decorators also can be valuable in figuring for you the exact amount of material needed. This can save you money. Many people order more than they need for fear that they'll run short of material when the drapes are being made up for them.

In addition to that, our own workshops make the drapes for many of the area's lovelier homes. They make the drapes, install the fixtures, and do the hanging for you. You'll be delighted with their thrifty charges.

One other thing, Mrs. Blue. The Accounts Department tells me that you don't have the convenience of a charge account with us. When you purchase your drapery material, and if you make use of our workshop, a charge account will make these transactions much easier and pleasanter for you.

So please accept this as a cordial invitation to apply for an account. With this letter you'll find a charge account application form, a folder describing the various types of credit available to you, and an addressed, postage-free envelope. Check off the type of account you want, fill in the required information and just drop it in the mail.

My warmest thanks for your interest.

Cordially,

Notice how this letter flows. There is not a single full stop in the continuity of thought. Even though the writer brought up four subjects, all four are linked together so naturally and smoothly they read as one. The second, third, fourth, and fifth paragraphs start with "connectors" that make the road smooth from start to finish.

Don't let extra messages become detours. When you introduce additional thoughts in your letter, you face the danger of putting ruts in your road and you also face the danger of providing detours.

Mrs. Blue, in the store's letter, was told that she could still get the drapery materials at the advertised price. That's fine. That's what she wanted to know. Now, along comes a new thought. She can get a trained decorator to come out to her home and give her professional advice and that service is free. Great! Up comes another thought. The workshop will make and install her drapes at thrifty prices. Splendid! One more thought: She is invited to open a charge account. Wonderful!

The letter was written in a manner that forged these individual thoughts into a strong, solid chain. That's how it must be done. But the same ideas, handled with less skill, could have fought one another. Each could have created a distraction, drawing Mrs. Blue's mind away from the others. The result would have been a confusion of offers and a confused Mrs. Blue.

Tie all the elements together. Confine your extra suggestions to those that relate to the basic issue. The writer would have made a grave mistake if the letter had included a message about a sale of dresses. Mrs. Blue is concentrating on drapes. The news about the dress sale may be exciting, but it will be irksome to her at this time. The letter, as it stands, is offering various types of practical help for the problem she is facing.

The advice of a dress sale would be pure selling and could pour cold water on her gratitude for the store's helpful attitude. It could do worse. It could woo her attention away from the drapery question to such an extent that she would fail to recall the good services offered.

It is entirely proper and logical to try to sell Mrs. Blue something else *provided that the something else is related to the main issue.*

When nonrelated thoughts must be introduced. Nothing in life is perfect. Despite a full appreciation that nonrelated items can hurt your letter, there may be times when you feel compelled to introduce them. It is a dangerous thing to do, but if you are aware of the danger you can take steps to minimize the ill effect.

Always return to the key topic. A good letter is like a circle. You start out with something, you bring up a second point, you return to the basic thought. You have completed your circle. You have reminded the reader of the key topic and have thus eliminated the danger of the secondary issue looming bigger and more important.

To demonstrate how this works, let's assume that you are an executive of a casualty insurance company. Your policies are sold by independent agencies. In your mail you have a letter from Brenda Bowen, one of your agents. She asks about the payment of a claim filed by her on behalf of one of her clients. On that particular day you had planned to write to the agent. You wanted to call her attention to a new way of selling your policies.

Dear Brenda,

The claim you filed for Mrs. George W. Knight has been processed. I spoke to our claims manager a few moments ago. He told me that they found it necessary to check some of the details with the accident investigation unit of your Police Department before they could pay the claim. This has been done. Everything is in order and by tomorrow night Mrs. Knight's check should be in the mail.

My compliments to you for watching out for your assured's rights so conscientiously. You reveal the interest in her well-being that marks a successful agent.

And it is that interest in the welfare of your clients that tells me you will welcome a new method of handling premiums we are about to inaugurate.

Starting the first of next month you are authorized to offer any of our policies on a six-month basis. Your clients will pay nothing extra but it permits them to have the same fine protection they enjoy today while tying up only half as much cash.

Although you'll have to handle renewals twice as often, you'll find that there are many advantages to you in this new procedure. You'll be in an excellent position to sell added types of protection because there is less cash to be paid out at any one time. You'll also find that the opportunity to see your clients twice as often can and will create added opportunities for you to know them better and to serve their insurance needs more completely.

When you get Mrs. Knight's check and deliver it to her, tell her about this new opportunity. This will give you a chance to see how welcome the six-month policy will be to those you serve now. And while Mrs. Knight is feeling good about getting the Company's check, you have the circumstances that are ideal to induce her to suggest some friends who need your services and would like the idea of advancing just half the customary amount of cash to get such splendid insurance protection.

Sincerely,

In this letter, the two unrelated thoughts have been woven together. This was done where the new thought was first introduced. It was done again when you returned to the original topic, completing the circle.

Bringing a series of ideas into one letter. The more that conditions require the introduction of a variety of thoughts into a single letter, the more adroit you must be in blending the elements.

Let's go overboard. We'll assume that you are a jobber of silverware, jewelry, and gift items. You send catalogs to stores in your territory and the retailers sell to their customers from the catalogs. You get a letter from one infrequent customer ordering a small item. Because this is an infrequent customer, you have not kept him posted on things that have developed since he received your catalog a number of months ago. In acknowledging his order you have a variety of things to bring to his attention.

Dear Mr. Storer,

The silver water pitcher, Item 702, will be shipped to you within five days. Thank you for the order and for your check covering the purchase.

Your order for that silver pitcher shows your appreciation of the profits you can enjoy when you sell merchandise from our catalog. And because

you realize that I thought you'd like to know about some steps we've
taken since you received the current issue of our big wholesale catalog.
Just take a look at these extra-profit helps you can enjoy.

Because of numerous requests, we have made it possible for you to
order one-page reprints of any parts of our catalog. Use them as
statement enclosures; for direct mail; for distribution in your store.
They will carry your name and address and are available to you at
our actual cost: only $18 per thousand.

More than 50 new items of wanted merchandise have been added to
our line since the catalog was released. Supplementary catalog
pages are enclosed covering all of these new items.

An excellent source of volume business is available to you, if you will
contact local clubs and church groups. You can offer to help them in
their fund-raising activities by staging gift-buying parties for them.
At such a party you will have a number of our catalogs on hand. The
members can order from the catalogs and you can share your profit
with the organization. Many of our retailer—customers have tried
this and have enjoyed excellent volume and have won the goodwill
of many people in their communities. If you want more information
on the handling of these parties, let us know. We'll show you just
what to do. Of course these are most successful when staged just
before Christmas and in the spring.

We are now equipped to monogram silver and leather goods for you.
With this letter you'll find a small folder showing the styles and
prices. This gives you the opportunity to offer fuller service and to
enjoy some additional profits.

As you can see there are many opportunities to increase your volume
and your profits through taking advantage of these various services.

When the silver water pitcher arrives, I hope that both you and your
customer will be as pleased as we are that we are working together.

Sincerely,

The physical arrangement of the letter is the key to its unity. If the
same items had been presented in the conventional manner the appeal
to the reader would have suffered. The letter would have been a series
of nonrelated paragraphs, each fighting with the others for interest.

Through the use of starred or indented paragraphs you are saying
that these are unrelated items, but that behind each one is a single
purpose: extra profits for the reader.

The need to take great pains to enable readers to follow a well planned sequence of thoughts may go beyond the letter. A letter is frequently accompanied by other printed matter. This is most likely the case if there is too much detail to put all of it in the body of the letter itself. You can see the challenge. If there is that much information to be conveyed, there is grave danger that readers may get lost, become confused and lose interest. Not only is it essential, therefore, to plan the fact-filled literature to make certain that prospects cannot stray from the path of clear and understandable logic, but the letter can also play an important role.

This brief letter paved the way to a guided tour of a complex enclosure:

Thanks for asking about our IRA Plan . . . .

There are several facts to be weighed. To make your consideration of those facts free of needless complications, this packet has been organized to present the story in logical, convenient order.

First, you will read the details of the IRA Plan and what it can accomplish for you. You then will turn to a discussion about putting your IRA dollars to work. There are four investment choices with varying objectives. You will discover that as your circumstances and objectives change, you may shift your accumulating assets from one to another that is more suitable at that time. It is a cost-free exchange.

Finally, there is the Application Form to start your personal IRA Plan now.

When accumulating money that can make such a vital difference in how you will live in your retirement years, time is critical . . . time is irreplaceable. I urge you to make your decision to take advantage of the tax-favored IRA Plan today. Harness every day available to you by acting now.

Sincerely,

MAIN CONSIDERATIONS IN YOUR EFFORTS TO MAKE YOUR LETTERS FLOW SMOOTHLY

1. Keep the reader on the road by removing stumbling blocks.

2. Use the first words of each new paragraph to link it to the former paragraph.

3. Eliminate all full thought stops in your letters.

4. Use extra messages in your letter as supporters of the main issue.

5. Blend all of your thoughts together.

6. Try to relate extra offers to the main issue.

7. Always return to the main issue.

8. Use physical appearance to blend nonrelated items.

9. Let the letter guide the reader to the logical way to absorb the facts in fact-filled enclosures.

Maybe there should be a . . .

VICE-PRESIDENT-IN-CHARGE-OF TODAY'S MAIL

Several chapters of this book include references to the importance of speed. That is a mistake. *Every* chapter should stress that critical factor. When people write to you, or your company, when they order something, subscribe, join, contribute, inquire, complain, or cancel, every day that goes by without their hearing from you hurts you. Each day of delay costs.

Recently I received a mailing offering a subscription to a monthly review and analysis of good mailings being employed by a variety of advertisers. If I accepted and sent them my $45 promptly I would be given a bonus: a collection of the best issues of recent years. Since I'm always eager to learn of innovative forms of mailed persuasion, I bought.

A month and half later I wrote to the publisher. I asked that my money be refunded. I told him that I had lost all faith in their ability to select what was good in mail order and direct mail since they were guilty of the worst crime a mailer can commit. Having received my money they forgot me. They had let six weeks go by without sending me *anything.* They had not delivered their publication; they had not mailed the promised bonus; they had not said, "Thanks for subscribing;" they had not said that there was some reason for delay.

More weeks went by before I received a surly note telling me that I should not expect a new subscription to be entered in their computer system in fewer than six to eight weeks.

If it takes six or eight weeks for them to get me into their computer, that's *their* problem. My problem is that I'm human. I resent it when I am ignored. When somebody asks, "Will you buy from me?" and I agree, I expect *some* response long before a month and half have gone by. If those arrogant people had used about 15 cents out of my $45 to send me a form postcard thanking me and telling me when to expect my first issue everything would have been fine. I could have become a steady, long-term subscriber . . . a booster. Instead, I'm a vigorous vocal knocker.

How often have you been the victim of similar discourteous indifference? Frequently, I'm sure, for this is one of the most widespread blindspots in marketing and customer relations.

Injured egos are only one portion of the damage done when people are subjected to such unthinking treatment. You mail a check or credit card authorization and then you wait. You hear nothing and receive nothing. *Did your payment get lost? Did it fall into the wrong hands? Are you going to get what you ordered and paid for? Can these people be trusted? Do you want to do business with them? Do they really want to do business with you?* Once they had their money they suddenly stopped being the smiling, cheerful people they had appeared to be during the courtship stage. You feel *deceived, ripped off, foolish, and insulted.*

Am I exaggerating the importance of this blind spot?

I'll tell you why it is not an exaggeration. It costs a lot of money for any type of business to locate, interest, and sell. Each newly acquired customer represents a substantial investment. Advertising people talk about "cost per inquiry." Those costs, normally, range from a few dollars to three figures. And that is just for an *inquiry.*

After getting an inquiry, there follows the additional and inescapable high cost of conversion: inducing inquirers to become buyers.

Money, effort, and genius are poured into the inquiry/sales campaign. And then, if those expensively acquired new customers are subjected to long-term indifference and neglect, while the gladiators turn their backs and go forth to do battle for more new customers, the acquisition costs zoom to ridiculous new heights . . . ridiculous because they are unnecessary.

Not everyone acts to demand immediate refunds as I did, but a heaping measure of resentment and mistrust have been implanted. Those seeds take root and will grow. When the time comes for a campaign to get those people to reorder or renew and the advertiser, once again, puts on the *"aren't we nice people"* mask, a needlessly high percentage are going to say, *"Thank you, but no thank you."*

The sin of getting around to customers and potential customers at the seller's convenience is not confined to the handling and recognition of orders. Letters of inquiry, seeking adjustment, explanation, and all the other things the public finds reason to write about, are subject to the same wholesale neglect. Nor is the cost of that neglect any less punitive than the examples just discussed.

Drawing, once again, on a personal experience, it took me just short of a full year and five letters to get a mail order firm I had bought a digital watch from to answer my question of how and where I could get it repaired. While my letters remained unanswered, several issues of their luxurious, four-color catalog came to our home. Every one of them hit the waste basket with a thud. Previously, we had been good customers.

Yes, it just might be a good idea to have a vice-president in-charge of today's mail. Today's mail should be answered today; tomorrow at the latest. Somebody with authority should have the responsibility to make certain that orders are acknowledged and letters are answered that quickly. It is a positive way of cutting costs, increasing profits, winning customer loyalty, and proving that you really are nice people.

The most customary reasons given for delayed replies are that there is too much mail to be handled that swiftly and that it takes time to get the name of a new subscriber or buyer integrated into the system. Let's examine those reasons.

WHEN YOUR IN TRAY OVERFLOWS

If you are convinced that it can be important and profitable to have all mail answered on a *today-or-tomorrow-at-the-latest* basis the chances are that one question comes to mind . . . how? How does anyone manage to adhere to such a policy when the in basket consistently overflows?

First, consider the fact that if responses now go out three to four weeks after receipt, you, and others in your organization, will be just as busy three or four weeks from now as you would be if you answered all of that correspondence today. *But first you must catch up.* During the next few weeks, devote whatever extra time is needed to clean out the backlog until you are current. From then on the methods that follow, if put into practice, will help you to remain current.

A. Mail on the Executive's Desk

As an executive your time is valuable. Here are six things you can do to handle the mail in your IN basket with economy of time, efficiency, and effectiveness.

1. Put an end to the greatest time waster of all: stop handling your mail more than once. It is common practice for busy, dedicated executives to quickly review their mail and then to handle it a second time to pull out the more important items ... to shuffle through the remainder several additional times to be certain that nothing urgent has been overlooked, again and again. So, the first rule is: *Make final decisions the first time you pick-up each item.* Each piece belongs in one of 5 categories. The first is Priority mail. These are the particularly important, sensitive, opportunity items that require immediate, personal replies. The other four categories follow;

2. "Jot it down" replies. Certain letters, particularly interoffice, or intercompany mail, can be answered with a hand written note right on the correspondence you receive. Your message should be written on the letter or memo when you first read it. Sales rep. Peters writes asking if he may give a certain customer a special discount. You write on his memo, "Okay this time only. Stay well, Pete." That is all the answer ... all the handling needed. It is out of your way and Pete's answer is on its way.

3. A standard letter will serve perfectly for your response to many letters. A "standard" letter is not the same as a "form" letter. A form letter has been preprinted and is used as is or a personalization is typed in. A standard letter is one that has been *composed* and is typed individually each time it is used, sometimes with pertinent dates, figures, or names dropped in at appropriate places. Many users of standard letters keep a book of them classified by subject and carrying identifying code numbers. The executive, dictating replies to the mail, simply says, or notes on the letter, the code for the response

to be sent, plus any detail to be inserted. It is a valuable time-saver. It also is one way of being certain that your replies are as good as they can be, for it is customary to have the standard letters composed with an exceptional amount of thought and care, as opposed to letters dictated under pressure.

4. Delegate. Answers to a good number of letters you receive should be routed to others . . . specialists in the subjects covered. These should carry either of two notations: "To be answered by Mary Teller, over her signature. Copy to me by noon tomorrow," or, "To be answered by Harry Mason for my signature by noon tomorrow."

5. Your secretary can play a key role in the campaign to vastly reduce the amount of time you spend on correspondence, and in getting answers on their way as rapidly as they should be. As mail arrives, he or she does the first screening. Certain letters and company memos can be answered by your secretary with a phone call, a hand written memo on the letter, or with a standard letter, to be prepared and presented for your signature. In some instances your secretary should compose replies, subject to your quick review and signature, and some can go over his or her own signature, requiring none of your time at all. There will be some letters where it will be clear that you will need some special facts or figures and these should be researched and provided via a note attached to the original letter, making it quick and easy for you to compose the letter of reply. Your secretary will also shoulder the responsibility of seeing to it that all of the replies you delegated on the previous business day have been written, that the copies, or the letters you are to sign, are on your desk when they should be.

6. The importance of correspondence, and the need to handle it with dispatch demands that your attention to it be programmed. It should not be a task to be tackled when other pressures permit. Your own experience, once you have applied the time-conserving concepts above, will establish the average amount of time needed each day. If one hour, for example, proves to be the time needed, determine which hour of each day is to be devoted to the mail and permit no ap-

pointments, unscheduled visitors, or phone interruptions during that period.

B. Acknowledgments of Subscriptions, Orders, Donations, Memberships

1. Subscriptions. There is no reason for the routine handling of these instant acknowledgments to make any demands on executive time. A routine should be established and religiously maintained. A simple, nonpersonalized printed postcard generally is sufficient. Here is a typical, well composed example:

> 30th CENTURY Magazine welcomes you.
>
> Thank you for subscribing. Before long I believe you'll be thanking yourself. In the months ahead you will be ahead of most of the people you meet. In discussions of the critical business, economic, and political problems that confront us you will have facts that very few others will have read or heard.
> Your first issue of 30th CENTURY will be in your hands in about three weeks.
>
> Gratefully,

2. Orders for merchandise: Establish a "flag" system. If an order exceeds a certain dollar amount, the answer should be a personalized letter signed by an executive. It should be one of a selection of standard letters composed for that purpose. There must be more than one such letter, since it would be counterproductive to send a good and consistent customer the identical thank you letter each time a purchase order is received. The customer's record, whether it be a card or in the computer, should show which letters have been sent and on what dates.

   All orders below the "flag" amount can be handled with nonpersonalized cards, letters, or printed forms. Even if it takes a hand-written fill-in, the acknowledgment should tell when shipment will be made.

3. Donations and memberships. Here, again, the "flag" system can be used. If the donation amounts to or exceeds a pre-

determined figure, if the membership application covers a certain number of individuals, branches, or offices, the importance of a personalized response is evident. All others should be acknowledged with an attractive enthusiastic letter spelling out what the donation makes possible, the benefits a new member will enjoy. New members should be told of materials that may be on their way under separate cover, as well as facts about forthcoming publications and meetings.

4. None of the acknowledgments described above should be postponed while waiting for computer or any other form of automatic addressing. The material should be on its way the day the subscription, order, donation, or membership is received. The cost of typing the names and addresses is an investment capable of yielding excellent dividends.

4

CAPITALIZE ON A "YES"

That's a silly subject to talk about, isn't it? If somebody asks for something and you're willing to give it to them, nothing is simpler than saying, "Yes." They're bound to be happy, aren't they?

Not always.

A number of years ago my wife saw an ad. One of the department stores was featuring a three-wheel bike for only $20. Our little guy was just at the age when he was ready for one. It sounded like a terrific bargain so she hurried to the store. The bike looked like a fine value for the money and she bought it.

Two days later one of the rubber tires snapped off. Back went my wife and the bike to the store. She found the salesman who had waited on her, and he remembered her. He was extremely pleasant and assured her that there would be no trouble at all. He called his section manager over and explained the situation. This dignitary gave my wife an icy glare and snapped, "What do you expect for $20?" Then to the salesman, "Give her a new one." With that, he stormed away.

Make the most of a "Yes." He said, "Yes." He backed up his company's policy of taking care of unsatisfactory merchandise. It cost them money to do it, and he handled it so curtly that he gave his firm a dividend for that expense: a lost customer. He had the great satisfaction of putting the customer in her place—only the place he put her in was a competitive store.

The reason it's important to talk about how to say "Yes" is because saying it is entirely too easy. Even when such extremes of stupid ill-temper are avoided in a letter, agreeing to a customer's request is so simple that you may neglect to do it as well as possible.

You think, "She asked for something and we gave it to her. Why make a production of it? Naturally she's happy. She likes us because we agreed. Why go further?"

There are several good reasons for going further.

In many cases when people ask for something, they make the request not *hoping* you'll agree; they are firmly convinced that they are absolutely entitled to what they are requesting. When you agree to such requests, the recipient has no reason to feel elated and to make a point of telling everyone they meet that your company is terrific—a great firm to deal with. They have no reason to feel particulary grateful or increasingly loyal to you. All they got was what they expected. And that represents a lost opportunity.

Saying "Yes" can cost but it can pay dividends too. When you agree to do or give something, it costs your company something in time, effort, or cash. Why not see a return on the investment? Why not say, "Yes," in such a way that the individual reads your letter with a growing smile and ends up saying, "What really nice people these are!"

That's the thing you're always shooting for and what greater opportunity have you than when you grant a request?

A "Yes" letter can be brief. A friend of mine received a wonderful "Yes" letter. He asked for something and expected his request to be granted, but the reply was so simple and so effervescent with a desire to serve that he was delighted.

This friend had bought a power lawn mower. He had it only a short time when the handle snapped. He called the store where he'd bought it, and they told him he'd save time by communicating with the factory, which is all they would do. He took the address and wrote to them.

Three days later he had a reply. It contained two delightful sentences.

> "New handle on the way. Throw yours in the ash can."

Isn't that wonderful? No explanation or stuffy expressions. Just solid, fully satisfying facts, cheerfully stated.

Say "Yes" in a hurry. When you write a letter asking for something and get a reply, you're eager. You want to know what they're going to do for you. You don't want to wade through a lot of meaningless conversation before you learn that you're getting what you ask for. If you are compelled to wait, your frame of mind keeps slipping down notch after notch. Finally you get the news you wanted. By that time you're relieved but annoyed because of the worrisome suspense.

So here is rule number one for saying "Yes," *say it graciously.* Rule number two is *say it immediately.*

Give more than they expect. That's the third rule. Many years ago my wife and I bought a Gibson refrigerator. Everything was fine until a big jar fell in it one day and cracked a glass shelf. We contacted the store, but they didn't have a replacement and talked as though it might take a few months. That didn't give us much satisfaction, so I dug up the address of the manufacturer and wrote a letter. The answer that came to us was so gratifying I'm still talking about it years later.

Back came this answer in a hurry.

Dear Mr. Nauheim,

A new glass shelf is being forwarded to you today. The arrangements we have with our dealers don't permit us to sell it to you direct, but we wanted you to have it as quickly as possible, and I'm sure he would too. That's why we expressed it right to you. Later on he'll send a bill.

I'm really very grateful to you for writing. We want you to get the greatest possible service and enjoyment from your Gibson Refrigerator, and an accident like that can be very annoying.

And by the way, Mr. Nauheim, since the model you have came out we developed something new. You know those two vegetable fresheners at the bottom? We found that a plastic cover for each of them helps keep your vegetables even crisper. So we developed a set of easy to handle plastic lids. I've had two of them put in with your new glass shelf. Please accept them with my compliments.

Very truly yours,

Did you ever hear of nicer people? Here I am telling whoever reads this book what a swell outfit Gibson is—how nice it is to have them behind you when you buy one of their products. And I've told it to many other people. So has my wife.

I've just got an idea that the few cents those lids cost them could mean several thousand dollars worth of business over the years. That's mighty economical advertising, isn't it? And all because somebody at Gibson's plant believes in giving a customer more than they expect.

They've done you a favor. Obviously it's wasteful and silly to grant a request and make the asker feel like an out-at-the-seat panhandler for having asked. That's something to avoid. But you can do more than avoid it. You can take a positive approach and go overboard in the other direction.

The fellow who wrote the Gibson letter did. He thanked me for giving them the opportunity to keep a customer pleased with their product. I can't think offhand of any cases where you can't find some reason to be pleased that you were asked for something you are in a position to give. Get excited about it, wax enthusiastic. It should and it can be genuine. After all, we're all human. We all like to feel important. There are few things anyone can do that makes us feel more important than granting a favor. So do be grateful, and show it in the tone of your letter.

The reader's interests come first. Reveal that and you made a lifelong friend. Are you a Scrabble® player? Thousands of people have found the game fascinating. It has been astoundingly successful. Perhaps one element of its success has been the attitude assumed when responding to a letter of inquiry by the people who market Scrabble.®

A Scrabble® player wrote the distributor, Selchow & Richter Company. In her letter, the customer said that she and her husband were avid Scrabble® players. They had owned a magnetic board and played the game so much that the board had become rusty and disfigured. Was there some way they could get a new board only, for the tiles and racks were still in good shape.

This was the reply:

Dear Mrs. Levy:

The magnetic edition of Scrabble® brand crossword board game has not been made for years. Replacement and game boards are no longer available.

But there is a way to renovate them. Enclosed are a couple gamesheets to get you started playing again.

If you will put a damp cloth over the rusty printed sheet, you will be able to peel it off after awhile. Although the steel liner underneath had been treated to be rust-resistant, salt spray or high humidity may have corroded it. Burnish it with steel wool to remove the spots. If you have some aerosol or solvent paint around the house, coat the steel liner to help it resist further rusting. Apply white glue or rubber cement to the back of the gamesheet and carefully position it over the steel backing.

Overnight your magnetic gameboard will look like new.

The magnetic edition is a lot of fun and easy to carry around. If you play it on a boat, try to keep it away from salt spray. Even though the water evaporates, the salt is insidious. It continues to attack the metal underneath.

Since you enjoy playing Scrabble® crossword game, we thought you would like the enclosed special word list and strategy hints on how to become an even better player of The Game.

Very truly yours,

SELCHOW & RICHTER COMPANY

Rose Cusimano
Customer Service

A king-size extra dividend! These folks aren't content with sending their public a pleasant "Yes" response. They say, in effect, "We don't want to see you spend your money to buy a new board when we can give you a way of rejuvenating your board for nothing."

Bad business? I don't think so. What a booster they've made out of Mrs. Levy, of me, perhaps of you. Can you put a price tag on those values?

There are four rules then for saying "Yes." Say it graciously. Say it right away. Say it with an extra dividend. Say it with enthusiasm.

"Yes, we were wrong." This is another type of letter. A busy florist had an unusually good customer, a large printing plant. It was the printing company's custom to send flowers to customers and employees whenever they knew of a birthday, anniversary, or any other special occasion. One afternoon they phoned an order.

The person who placed the order said, "I'm terribly late with this and you'll have to hurry. I just learned that one of our important accounts is leaving this evening on a second honeymoon trip. Send an extra nice orchid to his wife and put my card in with it, but you'll have to rush. They leave their home within an hour."

That was the night the florist's truck broke down. The corsage was never delivered.

The customer was angry. In his anger he forgot all the faultless service he had enjoyed for years. He would listen to no excuses. He was through, and he said so in unmistakable terms. The following day, although it was mid-winter, a beautiful bunch of lilacs were delivered to the irate customer's home. With it was a brief note from the florist:

Mr. G ——————,

These are winter blooming lilacs.
Very rare. Very, very rare.

The account came back.

A yes that puts the reader at ease. Raymond, James & Co. investment dealers in St. Petersburg, Florida found this in the mail one day.

Dear Mr. James,

I apologize for presuming on you for I have never been a customer of yours, and I never can be more than a nuisance account if I happen to make any investments. I have very little to invest.

Because my means are limited I feel I have to be extra conservative and examine any possible investment with unusual care. Friends have been talking about the ——————— Natural Gas securities and they sound attractive. What I would like is your opinion and a copy of their statement and any other papers you can give me that can help me to make up my mind.

If what I am asking is too much trouble I'll understand.

Very respectfully,

Mrs. J———M———————

The day the letter was received, this reply went in the mail.

Dear Mrs. M ———————

With this letter I am giving you our own analysis of ———————
Natural Gas, a Standard & Poor's report on the security, the company's prospectus, and their latest quarterly report.

We're more than happy to supply you with this information. Our only regret is that you seemed hesitant about making the request.

Helping people, giving them dependable information; those are the most important roles we fill. The amount you plan to invest and where you eventually take that investment are far less important.

Thank you for letting us help, Mrs. M _____, and please accept this warm invitation to visit us or to permit us to visit you. When we meet and discuss your situation fully we will be able to give you a much greater and fuller service.

Sincerely,

Robert A. James

The lady came in. Over a relatively short period of time her investments amounted to more than $150,000.

The "Yes and No" Letter

The "Yes and No" letter can be called preventive medicine. It is a handy type of letter to write when you agree to do something but don't want to establish a precedent. You say, "Yes, but never again."

Such a letter calls for elements of the "No" letter (the subject of the next chapter) and elements of the "Yes" letter. They are easy to blend. You start by rushing to tell correspondents that you will do what they ask. You then serve a sandwich with a meaty filling of reasons why, from their standpoint, you won't do it again. You conclude by giving them something extra.

Here's a good example.

A large national trade association conducts occasional campaigns to attract new members. In doing so they list an outline of advantages members enjoy. As the result of one campaign they enrolled a new member who read into the list of advantages more than was intended. The association said that they helped members with their tax problems.

A few weeks after the new member had joined he sent them a big parcel. In it were his books and records for the year. He asked them to figure his taxes for him. In his covering letter he siad he had joined because they offered this service. This was their reply:

Dear Mr. L_____,

Your completed tax return will be sent to you in a few days. It is being prepared now by our tax expert. Thanks for asking us to do this for you. It gives us the welcome opportunity to feel that we are very much a part of your team and that's a feeling we like.

When we prepare literature for a membership campaign we bend over backwards in an effort not to oversell. We do our utmost to tell you all the benefits of belonging to our association without exaggerating. There are so many solid reasons for belonging such tactics are far from necessary.

Once in a long while, however, we learn that we have been guilty of not making ourselves clear. This is such a case.

When we said, in the literature you read, that we have a tax expert on our staff to help members with their tax problems, we should have gone further. The fuller explanation would have pointed out that his job is to answer members who have specific questions about tax laws and regulations as they apply to them. But we did fail to be clear and you, with justification, believed we meant that we would handle all your tax work for you.

It would be a fine thing if we could offer such a service. However, as you can appreciate, if all our thousands of members did call on us for the preparation of their reports, we would have to hire a huge staff. To do so would require a substantial increase in your membership dues.

Because we were misleading we are happy to perform the service for you this year and we're grateful for having this weakness in our literature made clear to us. It will be corrected.

When your tax reports are forwarded to you I have suggested that our tax man also send you his actual work sheets. These will show how he handled the report and you'll find they will be very helpful to you in future years.

Your Association has many services to offer you. I hope you'll take full advantage of all of them.

Cordially,

This clever writer said "Yes," in a hurry and said it graciously. The writer thanked the member for the opportunity to serve him and thanked him again for bringing a weakness in their literature to their attention. The writer fully explained why such work could not be done regularly. He or she explained it from the viewpoint of the member by pointing out that the member's dues would have to be boosted if tax preparation was a membership privilege. The writer said "Yes and no" with great effect.

THINGS TO REMEMBER WHEN CAPITALIZING ON A "YES"

1. Never think that saying "Yes" is enough.
2. Saying "Yes" costs something, so be sure to get a return on your investment.

3. Say "Yes" graciously.

4. Say what you'll do immediately. Don't make readers dig.

5. If possible, give them something extra.

6. Thank readers for the opportunity to do something for them.

7. Say "Yes and No" by combining the needed elements for both types of letters.

5

IF YOU MUST SAY, "NO," SMILE

There are times when we must say "No" to friends, customers, and prospects. Obviously it is good business to say "Yes" whenever you can, but it is also good business to say "No" on many occasions.

"The customer is always right" is a brave statement that makes good reading and good telling, but it is not a true statement. Customers are often in error, and frequently to their own disadvantage. A successful businessman rephrased the statement. His motto is, "The right kind of a customer is always right." That comes closer to the truth, but it is filled with danger. It calls on you to sit in judgment on each customer and say, "This one is the right kind of customer. This one is not."

In personal contact selling, we meet our customers on frequent occasions and have the opportunity to assess them fully. We can measure them, test them: we can pass such judgments. As letter writers such opportunities are rare.

But even the right kind of a customer must be told "No" once in a while. Our job, right now, is to decide when and how to do so.

Your attitude writes the letter. Discussing any phase of letter writing, we invariably come back to that helium-filled word *attitude*. Here it is again.

Most often you are faced with the possibility of having to turn someone down when you've received a letter of complaint, a letter asking for adjustment, a letter asking for credit, or a letter asking for something extra. The attitude you take when you have read such a letter determines the nature of your answer. If the letter you read makes you indignant, scornful, suspicious, or unhappy and you retain that attitude while writing the reply, you will write a bad letter.

Most people are honest. Maybe I'm gullible, but I firmly believe that most people are fair and honest. Not all, but most. I have to believe that. I've had too many personal experiences in mass mailings to think otherwise.

Let me give you one example. I have a local client. He's a wholesale supplier of furniture, bedding, carpeting, and furnishings to hotels and large institutions. Some time ago we had a meeting. We discussed the fact that virtually no effort had been made to bring the firm's name to the attention of the motel and tourist home field. It was agreed that steps should be taken to correct that. The decision was made to map out a broad mailing campaign calculated to make the name of the firm well known to all tourist home and motel owners within our trading area. In order to get the ball rolling quickly, the very first piece had to be sufficiently sensational to make an indelible impression.

An idea was presented. There were many misgivings, much fear and trembling, but, at last, it was accepted. The company had a big supply of floor lamps in stock. They had been bought for $4.00 each from a bankrupt manufacturer. It was the type of lamp that the prospects could use to good advantage.

Here's what was done. A giant mailing card was prepared. It featured an illustration of the lamp and this was the headline: "You can have as many of these sturdy, metal floor lamps as you want for WHATEVER YOU CARE TO PAY. Do not pay more than $7.50."

That was really leading with the chin. You can understand the doubts, the worries, the misgivings.

What happened? Within two weeks the entire stock of some 2,500 lamps was sold at an average price of $6! Sure, there were a few chiselers who took advantage of the offer and bought some lamps for 25¢ each, but the vast majority paid a fair price and many paid the full price.

PEOPLE TRY TO BE FAIR

The reason I gave you that example is to establish a base: a base for your considerations when you receive a letter containing what might seem like an unwarranted beef or an unreasonable demand.

People want admiration. It's the nature of most people to want to appear to be fair, honest, and generous. They know that such types are admired. Everyone enjoys being admired. There is hardly anybody who doesn't like to be looked up to. If you are told, "So-and-so said you're a good person to deal with," you feel good. Everyone is susceptible to that kind of flattery. You are and so are the people who write to you.

When people become irritated or dissatisfied enough to write a letter of complaint, or to demand something, they pass up the opportunity to pose as, or to think of themselves as, the proud, generous type. Becoming complainers belittles them in their own esteem, and they do it with discomfort. They do it only when they feel that they have been deprived of something that rightfully is theirs. They are angry . . . hurt.

And people are lazy. People don't take the time and trouble to write letters of complaint or adjustment unless they are moved strongly.

Weigh the human values before saying "No." Take all the factors into consideration and you can't escape the conclusion that most letters of that type are written because the writers have powerful convictions that they are right. They may be 100 percent wrong, but they *think* they are right.

Sure, there are the chiselers. Chronic trouble-makers, the people who spend the better part of their lives writing letters to the editor and to City Hall. But, thank goodness, they're a small minority. You, as a letter writer, can't afford to make the error of letting the minority distort your vision of the majority. The safest, surest course is to assume that everyone you receive a letter from—no matter how distorted their logic—is a person who writes with full conviction that his or her cause is just. In most cases you'll be right.

And then turn to the Bible, "A soft answer turneth away wrath."

Perhaps you should say "Yes." If you are genuinely sympathetic to the writer's viewpoint, you are capable of writing a refusal that reflects that sympathy. Such a letter strikes a responsive chord. So the first thing to do when you receive a letter with a seemingly outlandish request is to sympathetically consider how and why the writer came to such conclusions. That puts you in a position to explain the reasons why it can't be done *from their standpoint*. It's just possible that some of the requests you normally would turn down should be granted. If that is the outcome of your reasoning, both the reader and your company gain. Even if it is out of the ordinary, if your decision is that the request or complaint is just, you make the customer happy and you advertise the fact that your organization is unselfishly interested in helping the individual fully and fairly.

But often you have to say "No."

WHEN YOU SAY, "NO," MAKE A SANDWICH

The top layer consists of something the reader wants to know, something pleasing.

The middle layer is a fat meaty filling of the reasons why you must refuse.

The final layer, like the first, is something pleasing, something you *will* do.

In a moment we'll elaborate on that sandwich. First let's put the POISON label on some of the common faults of refusal letters.

No need to offend. Avoid, like the plague, statements like, "I'm sorry, but it is against the company's policy to do what you ask." You might just as well say, "Me . . . I'm nice, but these heels I work for have some cockeyed rule that says you can't have it."

Never say, "You claim," or, "You state," or "According to you," or anything else of that nature. It can and will be interpreted as, "You're a liar." "I don't believe you." If the writer says that a shipment was received with several parts missing and you have cause to restate the case in your reply, which of these sounds better to you?

"You claim that several parts were missing."

or

"I understand that several parts were missing."

Start your letter with something good. Now we've returned to the sandwich. You've read and reread the letter and have decided that you must refuse the request. Think, despite my refusal, is there anything I can do, anything I can offer, anything I can say that will please this person? There's always *something*. Start your letter with the best of those somethings. Now you come to that big, ugly, "No."

You can say "No" and make most people like it by a full—a very full—explanation, and by demonstrating that the request was given a good deal of thought.

Explain a refusal in detail. The explanation of the reasons why has to be from the viewpoint of the majority of your customers. Show that the request was considered seriously, weighed, discussed. The consideration must regard the individual's request, not something that was examined a long time ago and then established as a general rule or policy.

Finally, you end up with that bottom layer of the sandwich. You end up with something you *will* do, or something very pleasing. The end of your letter is always the part remembered longest. It is the dessert course. You want to leave the reader with a good taste. Maybe, in some cases, you'll have nothing more pleasing to offer than the item you used for the top layer, the opening of your letter. In that case, restate it, rephrase it, remind the reader of the positive factor.

Refusal of long-term credit. Let's try a test case. Here is a letter received by the McGraw-Hill Continuing Education Center (NRI). They offer home study courses in electronics, television, radio servicing, electrical appliance servicing, automotive servicing, small engine repair, microcomputers and microprocessors, and air conditioning, refrigeration, and heating.

Dear Mr. Schek,

Well, I've just signed the lease and I'm opening my own radio and TV repair shop. Even though I haven't finished half the course yet, the practical experience I had before I started and what I've learned from you folks so far makes me feel I can make a go of it.

I guess that gives you some idea why I've gotten a little behind in my payments. I think I owe you for three months right now. It takes a lot of money to start a shop, fix it up, and get all the tools and equipment. I guess you know that.

Everybody's been very nice to me. The companies I approached have all agreed to give me credit even though I'm new and never did any business with them before. Well, you folks have known me for nearly six months now and until recently I've always paid on time. You know what can be made in this business and from the good grades and reports I've had on my assignments I think you know I have what it takes to make this business a success.

So I'm asking you to do what the people who don't know me have done. I want to complete the course just as fast as I can. The more I know the better I can do, but I want you to give me credit. I want to finish the course and make the payments later after the shop starts earning money.

Maybe six months from now, as much as a year at the most, I'll have an easy time paying. In the meantime keep me going and you can count on getting your money when I'm through. This will apply to the kits too. I've got to hold on to all my money for working capital.

I'll appreciate your cooperation.

Very truly yours,

John Johnson

The NRI has no financial arrangements that would make it possible for them to okay such a request. This was their reply:

Dear Mr. Johnson,

You are absolutely right. The assignments I've received from you, and the experience you have had, give me great faith in the success of your new enterprise. And don't worry at all about being behind on your payments for the past three months.

After reading your letter this morning I took it to Mr. Thompson's office and we discussed it at some length. We're both very pleased with your progress, your ambition, and the bright future you face. It was our conclusion, however, that we'd be doing you a great disservice if we did the easy thing and said "Yes," to your suggestion. We've seen lots of students start businesses of their own. Many made good but there are some who didn't. We want to see you make good.

It is never a good idea to start a business in debt. Credit is fine and useful. But normal credit generally means that you pay what is owed in thirty days time. If we agreed to your plan, you would be building up a debt for six months or a year. In time, despite how well your business might be doing, that debt would become a serious burden. It is not a healthy way to start. You are far better off if you keep yourself current, knowing what your fixed expenses are each month and meeting them. When you consider that I'm sure you'll agree that it is the only sound way to launch your new career.

Of course we know what a burden it is to start a new shop. For that reason, and because we want to help in every way we can, I have told the bookkeeping department to adjust the books so that you are on a current basis. The three months you owe for now can be paid for at the end of the course. That gets you off to a fresh, new start just like that new shop of yours.

To give you some additional help I'm enclosing one of our folders, "How to Open Your Own Shop." This is always sent to our students when they've completed the course, but I thought you'd find it helpful now. The best of good luck to you!

Cordially,

Joseph Schek

Read Mr. Schek's letter more than once. It is an exceptionally fine example of how to respond to a reasonably expressed request that asks you to go beyond good business practice. Put yourself in the student's situation. You put a lot of thought and effort into your letter asking for exceptional credit. You feel that you have stated your case well and that there is every reason for the school to cooperate in the manner you've suggested. And then you wait for the reply.

Now consider the reaction to the top layer of Mr. Schek's sandwich. In the nicest way you are told that you are right, that your work has been excellent, that the writer has great faith in the success of your new venture, that they will agree to the postponement of your payments for the past three months.

You have to like these people. Now you come to the meat of the sandwich. The way it starts, the opening of the second paragraph, is one of the strongest parts of the letter. Everybody likes to feel important. You feel important when you learn that Mr. Schek thought that the things you said were important enough to justify his going to the top executive of NRI to discuss your request. From that point on, you are following the reasoning of people you like. And everything said, even though it is not exactly what you wanted, reflects consideration of what is best for you.

The final layer to the sandwich brings welcome news. You have been given a booklet full of ideas and facts that can help you to establish your new business now, no waiting until the end of the course.

Of course you regret that you failed to get everything you wanted, but regrets and bitter anger are far apart. You take a deep breath and you buy the concept that they probably are right.

You can refuse with a smile. The credit manager of a women's apparel shop received a letter asking for a charge account. A routine check showed that the applicant had accounts at several other local stores and was not meeting her obligations. The manager had to refuse the application but wanted to keep her good will. Some day the customer may be a good credit risk; meanwhile she can be a cash customer.

Dear Mrs. Applier,

You've paid us a high compliment in applying for a charge account. You've given us your confidence and have shown that you like our selections. I have something I'd like to give to you.

Dealing with people—their finances and their budgets—day after day, makes me something like an expert I suppose. Many, many times I've had the real pleasure of helping people who have become tangled up in financial problems.

When your application arrived we asked the local credit bureau for the usual report. I have just spent quite a while carefully reviewing the report, and I am convinced that it would not be wise for you to take on added obligations at this time. That's why I'm making this letter an invitation.

Why don't you visit with me the next time you're in the store, Mrs. Applier? Perhaps, from the variety of experiences I have had helping people with money matters, I might be able to give you some thoughts that could prove valuable to you. I'll be delighted to be of assistance, and I'm sure the store shares my feelings.

Sincerely,

Credit managers are in an excellent position to give individuals a great deal of sound advice about budgeting. Perhaps they will see where a troubled person with many delinquent bills would be better off to consolidate their debts by securing a personal loan. But whether Mrs. Applier accepts the invitation or not it is logical to assume she will have a warm feeling toward the store that offers a sympathetic, helping hand, even though they did not give her credit.

Any time the credit manager devotes to such counseling can bring untold dividends in good will, customer loyalty, and priceless word-of-mouth advertising.

Saying "No" to a juicy prospect. A large manufacturer of drug products, with their own salespeople situated in the major cities, had a letter from the head of a big chain of drug stores. The chain never had bought from this concern. The current salesperson and those who had covered that territory earlier had made many efforts to win the account but had failed.

Now the president of the drug chain had written. He said he would like to take on the manufacturer's full line for all of his stores, but he wanted to buy direct, bypassing the salesman. If the manufacturer agreed, the chain would expect lower prices since there would be no sales commission to pay.

The offer was tempting, for the volume would be considerable. But this company protected its salespeople. They knew that they would be establishing a bad precedent if they agreed to the proposal. They would undermine the confidence and morale of their entire sales force. They had to refuse. This was the letter they wrote:

Dear Mr. P_____,

Every time Boston has been mentioned in these offices somebody has sighed and wistfully talked about your great chain of modern drug stores. You must be immensely proud of the progress you have made, for I know that the entire drug industry is grateful to you for the manner in which you have raised the prestige and public acceptance of our contribution to society.

As you know we have made many overtures over the years. It has been our ambition to count you as one of our distributors. For these reasons your letter found a warm welcome.

I think you'll be particularly interested in the observation made by our national sales manager when I called a meeting this morning to discuss your proposal.

Mr. Osgard said, "The proposal would be far more tempting if we didn't know our own salesmen so well. We have built this business and it continues to grow, not only because we are so careful about the uniform high quality of our products and the popular demand we have created with national advertising, but because every field man we have has been trained to help our retail customers to make extra profits.

"If we accepted this offer and eliminated the salesman we could reduce the prices but we'd be reducing Mr. P's turnover and profits too. These people are wonderful merchandisers but our men are specialists. They have never failed to show retailers how to make the most of our products, our promotions, our in-the-store merchandising. Our agreement to their offer would give them a surface advantage but would deprive them of a bigger, more important advantage. We'd be doing them a serious disservice."

What Mr. Osgard said is abundantly true. One additional consideration is that our business has been built on loyalty and good faith. We cannot violate these with our salesmen any more than we can with our customers.

Your business is so much to be desired it is difficult for me to reject you on any terms. If it suits your convenience I am planning to catch an early morning flight to Boston next Tuesday. I'll be delighted if you'll see me and our local representative, Mr. Hammond, at ten o'clock that morning. The timing is particularly appropriate, for we have news of a dramatic new national promotion about to be launched. When you hear the details I know it will appeal to your fine merchandising sense and you will see the broad opportunities for your own organization.

If the date I have mentioned is not convenient I'll appreciate your suggestion for a more suitable time.

My sincerest thanks for your letter.

> Cordially,
> Claude Snow, President

Mr. Snow got his appointment. He did not make a sale at that meeting, but did win the chain's business within the year. This letter was an important factor, for it led the drug chain's president to the inescapable conclusion that Mr. Snow's company stood for outstanding integrity.

There is a "no sandwich" with a fat filling of meat and a tempting aftertaste. The letter does much more than say, "No." It takes the negative, turns it completely around, and makes the reasons for the refusal powerful sales arguments.

Kalb, Voorhis & Co., a New York Stock Exchange firm, at one time produced a service for investment firms throughout the country. The service supplied the dealer firms and their salespeople with advertising and sales training materials. The firm offered a basic subscription to dealers plus supplementary kits for each of their salespeople. One morning's mail brought this letter from an organization that employed an exceptional number of salespeople.

Gentlemen:

Thank you for sending me samples of your MSS service. It looks quite interesting, and I can see where we could use it to excellent advantage. We are considering taking a basic subscription plus 86 salesmen's kits.

If we do take the service we will make full use of it. In other words we will be using your newspaper mats and sales letters and literature extensively. We cover our territory thoroughly and I would want your assurance that we will be given exclusive use of your material for this area before we enter into any agreement with you.

I look forward to your reply.

Sincerely yours,

R.M.S _____

Kalb, Voorhis & Co. did not offer the service on an exclusive basis. They answered Mr. A's letter in this manner.

Dear Mr. A _____,

Your interest in the MSS service is as fine a tribute as we could hope for. There are few retailing organizations in the country who have won and merited the reputation for progressiveness you enjoy. My sincerest thanks for your stamp of approval.

Your request that you be given an exclusive on MSS services for your area has been given a great deal of study. Your reasons for requesting it are clear and certainly make good sense. If you'll follow me through the reasons why this is impractical, however, I think you'll agree that it would not give you any true advantage.

If we were to accept subscriptions on an exclusive basis we would have far fewer subscribers. The only antidote for that, naturally, would be a considerable increase in the annual fees. The subscription price would be multiplied by four or more. Even that might be acceptable to you until you weigh the questionable advantages you would gain against the additional costs.

Don't you agree that the vastly higher fee we'd be compelled to ask for an exclusive on MSS would fail completely to bring you commensurate advantages?

And there's one thing more, Mr. A _____. When you subscribe to MSS you have the privilege of coming to us with requests for any special newspaper or direct mail advertising you want prepared for your individual use. Here you do have an exclusive. There's no charge for these services. We're delighted to do these things for you.

Since MSS does represent to you a sound tool for adding to your sales, and to the strength of your advertising and sales training, I hope that I have answered the one objection that came to mind in a manner that opens the doors for this great flow of invaluable services. They can start increasing your sales and profits next week if you'll phone me collect or mail your acceptance today.

Cordially,

Consider each of these examples of letters of refusal and you'll find in the background a uniform attitude, a genuine desire to help.

THINGS TO REMEMBER WHEN YOU MUST SAY "NO"

1. Your attitude writes the letter, so avoid anger and indignation.

2. First, put yourself in the writer's shoes.

3. Look for logical reasons for a complaint or unusual request even if they were not expressed.

4. Agree if you can.

5. Say "No" with care and thoughtfulness.

6. Avoid expressions that may create anger.

7. Start out with something the reader will like.

8. Take a lot of space and time to give your reasons for refusal.

9. Explain your rejection from the standpoint of the reader.

10. End your letter with something you will do or something of benefit to the writer.

PUT EXCITEMENT
IN YOUR LETTERS

Enthusiasm is catching. Every letter you write is a selling letter. At least it should be. Picture a wide-awake, up-on-his-toes, good looking personable salesman coming to see you. He tells you his story with all the gusto and zip he can command. He's so excited about his product or service you find yourself carried away. Some of that excitement has touched you. He's a powerful transmitter and you're a sensitive receiver. You receive his signal so well you want to go along with his suggestion no matter how little you want and need whatever he has to offer.

Compare an enthusiastic salesperson with your letters. Just visualize that kind of selling and the influence it has on people. Compare it with the letters you write. Compare it with *any* letter—the finest strongest letter ever written. There really is no comparison, is there?

The printed word just can't stand up next to the onslaught of a human being when that human being is virtually bubbling with excitement.

If you take that statement at face value, you might say, "I might as well quit writing letters if that's the competition." And since your letters are intended to sell, personal salesmanship is the competition, at least part of it. Every time one of your customers or prospects meets that kind of a salesperson, you're in danger of losing something. If the salesperson your customer encounters is capable of closing sales, the time may come when that customer no longer can afford to buy anything more from anyone, including you.

But there is a saving grace.

Despite all the books and all the lectures and the crystal clear logic behind the employment of enthusiasm in personal selling, most salespeople don't have it. No. Most people who call themselves salespeople are perfectly content to be mediocre. They tell their story in a dull, lifeless manner, in a bored monotone, without showmanship, fire, or bubbles. They give the listener the impression that they don't think the whole thing is very important and *that* thought, at least, they do succeed in selling.

It's strange, but it's true.

Most business letters lack enthusiasm. Reexamine your position as a letter writer. The weakness that exists in most salespeople is also present in many letter writers. They have certain things to say in their letter and they say them . . . period.

Since you have to overcome many mediocre salespeople and an occasional star salesperson, put enthusiasm in your letters. Make your letters star salespeople overflowing with excitement. If you do that, you can compete.

You have to be more enthusiastic than most salespeople, in order to overcome the handicap of doing your selling on paper and not in person. As a matter of fact, you have to be more enthusiastic than the really *good* salespeople to submerge that disadvantage.

IT'S WHAT YOU SAY, NOT HOW IT'S TYPED

Some people, with an appreciation of the need to make every letter exciting, make the effort by studding their typewritten sales stories with lots of capitalized words, lots of underscoring, and with dozens of exclamation points.

That's not the answer.

Convert that to personal selling and you'll see the amazing spectacle of salespeople screaming at the top of their lungs every time they want to make a point. They scream, pound the desk, and shove their noses right up against the prospects'.

There are several bad things about letters with a lot of capitalized statements and underscoring and exclamation points. They *look* bad, and are disruptive to the eye of the reader. While one part of your letter is being read, another portion tugs for attention. It's confusing and disruptive.

One glance at the letter says to the reader, "Someone is trying to pressure me into something."

Typewriter gymnastics destroy the personal quality of your letters. You know the importance of making your letters personal in tone and appearance. One way of accomplishing that is to make the letter read and look like a letter you might get from a friend. Maybe you do have one friend who uses typewriter gymnastics in social correspondence, but it isn't likely. Most people don't.

Nor can you put excitement in your letters by picking up a glossary of words that will make your letters more enthusiastic. There is only one thing that will do the trick, the same element that dictates all the other good qualities we've discussed: your attitude.

To write an enthusiastic letter, be enthusiastic. Lots of people say, "But I'm just not built that way. I'm a placid person. I have no bubbles. I never get excited about anything. If I try to sound enthusiastic in my letters, I'm putting up a false front. My letters become insincere. It isn't me talking."

All of which brings up the question: are people *born* with enthusiasm? Is it a quality we either have or don't have? Or is it something that can be developed and cultivated?

You can develop enthusiasm. That has been well established. Enthusiasm is an attitude. You know you can change your attitudes. Yes, some people seem to be born with enthusiasm and some without. Certainly the one who comes by it naturally will always have it to a greater degree than the one who develops it in later life, but that makes the development no less desirable.

Enthusiasm is a way of life. It is not just a way of selling, not just a way to write letters.

Everyone likes enthusiastic people. They inspire others. They are the leaders. They are the successful people of the world in business, the professions, the church, politics, socially, and at home. They are the happy people.

Enthusiasm brings achievement. There's something so alive, so vital, so stimulating about enthusiastic people, they win your confidence and your loyalties. Being near an enthusiastic person is a tonic; therefore, you want to be near such people more often. Enthusiasm gets things done. And because you get things done, because it makes you more likeable, because it makes everything you do more interesting and exciting, enthusiasm makes life more fun and more rewarding.

Just think of the most successful people you know. With few exceptions you'll realize that they are the most enthusiastic people you know. And no matter how little or how much enthusiasm you possess now, you can build it higher.

YOU ALWAYS CAN FIND A BASIS FOR GENUINE EXCITEMENT

When you accept the idea that your letters should be enthusiastic, you'll wonder how you'll apply the things we've seen discussing. It is easy. You are a conscientious person. That's a known fact. You wouldn't take the time to read this book if you were not. You have a job to do and you are willing to give some of your time to finding ways and means of doing your job better.

Because you are built that way you know that anything you offer to do for the people you write to is going to be done extremely well.

The chances are you believe in your organization. You are convinced that the products or services you offer are excellent. You have every reason to feel, when you get a letter of inquiry, for example, that you should be enthusiastically grateful to the writer. You can have warm feelings about the people you believe to be well qualified prospects for whatever you are promoting. If people weren't interested in what you offer, where would *you* be?

You have many reasons to be enthusiastic. And that's true even when you are replying to a letter of complaint. If the complaint is justified and you are going to make amends, you'll be enthusiastic about the service you offer, about the way your company backs up its customers, about the trouble the customer took to tell you when something was wrong.

The customer complained and gave you the opportunity to demonstrate the square dealing of your company. Had an unhappy customer remained silent and grumbled to others about the real or imagined problem, you could have been hurt.

A letter of refusal can be enthusiastic too. In the previous chapter you read how to say "No" with a smile. You learned that a sound way to write such letters is to start and end with something you will do for the customer or, at least, with something pleasing. There's plenty of room for enthusiasm when telling of such things. You can be enthusiastic when explaining, from the customer's viewpoint, why you must refuse.

Shannon & Luchs, one of the larger real estate firms in Washington, D.C., received this letter.

Gentlemen:

My company has just transferred me from New York City to Washington. I'll be coming to your city in thirty days. I am married and have three small children. My wife and I would like a home in a good residential area. We want a nice backyard where the children can play safely. We will require four bedrooms and at least two baths. My wife wants a modern kitchen and we want to be near a good school and handy to public transportation.

I'll be in Washington next Wednesday and Thursday and will call you when I get there. If you have anything meeting my specifications write and tell me and I'll contact you when I arrive. I'm willing to rent or buy, depending on what you have.

Sincerely yours,

R_____G_____

The reply had no excitement. Somebody in the sales department was given the letter and wrote a long letter describing four properties the firm could offer for sale. The letter was filled with detail about each house. It answered Mr. G's question but it was cold and dry.

The letter was placed on the desk of Mr. Kenneth Luchs, a highly successful enthusiastic salesman. He tore it up and wrote a new letter.

Dear Mr. G_____,

Unless you really know Washington you can't appreciate how happy you and your family will be living here. And you couldn't have written to us at a better time.

Washington is clean and beautiful. It is the most interesting city in the world. In and around the city there are a great many delightful residential areas. Each has so much to offer your only problem will be deciding which you like the best.

Bill Ellis, the head of our Residential Sales Division, is a native. He knows the city thoroughly. Mr. Ellis has assigned Gloria Thrasher, one of our best sales associates, to help you. He asked her to make a careful study of the many listings we have right now. She has your letter and will hand pick several homes that give you everything you want. She'll drive you to each and will give you the full benefit of her intimate knowledge of the areas so that you and Mrs. G_____ can make your choice on the basis of full knowledge. You'll see the nearby schools, the shopping areas, the public transportation and will learn what types of people you'll have for neighbors..

Thank you, Mr. G_____for giving us the welcome opportunity to establish you in this gracious city in a manner that will make this the happiest home you've ever had.

When you arrive next Wednesday just ask for Mrs. Thrasher. She's looking forward to meeting you.

Cordially,

Kenneth J. Luchs, President

Get the prospect excited. Mr. Luchs had a lot to offer to Mr. G_____. He knew it. He was enthused about it and he gave Mr. G_____ full opportunity to share that enthusiasm. It is hard to believe that Mr. G_____ would give a thought to asking any other real estate firms to help him in his quest for a home. *Enthusiasm sells.*

Even a reply to a complaint can be answered with enthusiasm. Enthusiasm will help any letter and the reply to a letter of complaint is no exception.

Ginns, retail stationers in Washington, received a letter of complaint.

Dear Mr. Marshall,

About two weeks ago we received one of your mailing pieces featuring your 60-minute delivery service. It sounded fine and we were impressed. The day before yesterday we had occasion to prepare a long, involved contract for one of our clients. About two in the afternoon I learned that we would not have sufficient paper to finish the job. I phoned your main store and ordered two reams of legal-size rag bond and 2 reams of second sheets. Twenty-four hours later they were delivered. In the hustle and bustle of getting the job done I didn't realize till after six in the evening that the supplies had not arrived and by then it was too late to do anything about it. We lost many precious hours.

I think that you should back up your advertising claims or leave well enough alone. Your ad led me to believe that you meant what you said, and you created a great deal of difficulty for us because you didn't.

We've been pretty good customers of yours for many years, and although this incident may not drive us into the arms of your competitors it surely is a push in that direction.

> Yours very truly,
>
> Helen C_____,
> Office Manager

Ginn's replied with this enthusiastic letter.

Dear Miss C_____,

The best friends we have are those who give us you-know-what when we need it. My deepest thanks for telling me what happened and my equally deep apologies.

And the whole thing is my fault.

I put my okay on the mailing card that told you about our 60-minute messenger service. You have pointed out a serious weakness in that card and that's one of the reasons why I'm so grateful to you. With this letter I'm giving you a copy of the card. I've circled in red the part that says, "When you want the 60-minute service please ask for 'Messenger Service.' " I can see now that this should have been much bolder.

The 60-minute service is brand new with us. We inaugurated it at the time you received the card just to take care of our good customers when they are faced with emergencies of the type you described. To be sure that anyone who wants this special service gets it, without question, we established a special order desk for 60-minute service calls.

When your letter came in this morning I did some quick checking. I found that your order was taken at the regular service desk, and I saw at once that I had fallen down in failing to stress to our customers that they should ask for Messenger Service.

Will you forgive me? Will you try the 60-minute service again—so that you can see how well it operates? We call it 60-minute service but you'll find that you'll get what you ask for in far less time than that.

Again, my heartiest thanks for telling me what happened and for making it possible for me to put the stress where it is needed the next time we pick up our megaphone to shout about this great new service.

> Cordially,
>
> M.S. Marshall

This letter, because of the enthusiastic expressions of appreciation and understanding, accomplishes a difficult diplomatic feat. Without ever saying it, the writer lets the customer know that the fault was hers, but the writer takes the blame.

An enthusiastic refusal. You may be sorry that you have to turn down a customer, but there is no need to let a tone of sorrow creep into your letter. You may not be able to make a sale today but you can stir up the reader's appetite for what you have to offer for the future.

As an example let's look at a letter from Summertime Haven, a New England resort hotel. They received a request to reserve accommodations for a family of four for one week beginning August 1st. This is the peak season for the resort and they're booked solid. This was the reply.

Dear Mr. L_____,

How I wish I could start this letter by telling you how happy John and I will be to see you again this summer. To my sincerest regret your request came too late. We are booked to the limit of our capacity for the entire season starting August 1st.

It would have been particularly wonderful to have had you with us again this summer. Many of your friends will be here then and we have so many new things John and I would like you to see and enjoy. Not the least of the new things is a marvelous chef we brought here from New York.

The boat and swimming docks have been completely rebuilt and we've added seven more canoes to the navy department. An additional tennis court has been built and many of the cabins have been entirely refurnished.

I've phoned around to a few of the more desirable places to see if they could put you up, but all of them are as overloaded as we are that week. I do hope you find something in the area, because we'd love to say hello to you and hope you'll drop in and be our guests for cocktails any day you are nearby.

With this letter I'm giving you one of our cards with the winter address. Please write real early next year, just as soon as you know when you can get away so that I'll never have to turn you down again. Being forced to tell you that we are full spoiled my day. I hope you have a wonderful summer.

                         Cordially,

                         Helen Glass

A refusal written in this manner increases the desire to stay at Summertime Haven in the future. A less enthusiastic reply could have offended a former guest.

Enthusiasm in the granting of a request. The Potomac Electric Power Company received this letter from a housewife.

Gentlemen:

My husband and I are planning to remodel our home. Our contractor has recommended an electric heat pump. We've never used anything but gas heat, and I hate the idea of having to learn how to operate a new system. Frankly, we're not too well advised on the advantages, if any, of the electric heat pump. Can you give me any information that will help us to make a decision?

Yours truly,

Mrs. G.L. H_____

The enthusiastic reply read:

Dear Mrs. H _____,

You are in for a treat. An electric heat pump has much to offer. It means a cleaner house, and year-round energy efficiency in a time of rising costs.

We'd like to tell you about the adventure lying before you. To do this, I'd like to make a date to come to visit you in your home. When I'm there I can look at your house and your plans for the renovation, and perhaps advise you about other ways to conserve energy.

If you'll take a look at your calendar to see when my visit will be best for you I'll phone you on Monday and we'll make the date.

I look forward to a very pleasant visit with you.

Cordially,

Larry Barrett

MAIN CONSIDERATIONS WHEN PUTTING EXCITEMENT IN YOUR LETTERS

1. The best salespeople are the enthusiasts.

2. Your letters must be enthusiastic salespeople.

3. Enthusiasm consists of genuine excitement, not typewriter gymnastics.

4. You can cultivate enthusiasm.

5. Look to yourself and to the company you represent when seeking a foundation for enthusiasm.

6. Be conscious of all the reasons why you should be enthusiastic.

7. You can be enthused even when you have to write a letter of refusal.

8. Be excited and your reader will be excited too.

ADD
A HEAPING MEASURE
OF CONFIDENCE

Old Silas went to his brother-in-law's funeral. The brother-in-law had been a very cautious man. Years before he died he had written the epitaph for his own headstone, had it prepared, and put in storage. When the body was lowered into the grave, old Silas put on his specs, creaked forward and read the tombstone. It said, "Here lies George Williams. He isn't dead. He is just asleep."

Silas straightened up and grunted, "Hmph! He ain't fooling nobody but himself."

We often make the same mistake when we write letters. If we exaggerate, if we stretch the truth, if we attempt to glide over rough areas in an effort to make them look smooth, we ain't fooling nobody but ourselves.

Confidence comes before a sale. Mr. Webster defines confidence as "that in which faith is put or reliance had."

There can be no progress made when two people meet, whether in person or through the mails, unless there is some measure of faith and reliance. The reader must have confidence in you as a person who speaks with knowledge, a person who is sincere and honest. The reader must have confidence in the belief that you are devoted to his or her best interests.

WHERE CONFIDENCE EXISTS ANYTHING CAN HAPPEN

Years ago, I attended a fascinating private demonstration at a radio station.

The purpose of the demonstration was to prove that people could be hypnotized by remote control. A well known New York psychiatrist had an idea for a new type of radio program. Many people have trouble sleeping at night. He wanted to introduce a late evening show. He would appear on the show and use his skill with hypnotism to make people sleep. It was quite an idea. The purpose of the demonstration that afternoon was to show that it could be done.

We met in a small studio of the radio station. About 20 of us were there. I knew everyone in the audience. There were no stooges.

First the manager of the station told us about the doctor's idea. He then introduced the doctor's assistant. This gentleman spent about 15 minutes filling us in on the doctor's professional achievements. He was one of the pioneers in the use of hypnosis in psychiatric treatment. We heard of some of the splendid cures he had effected through hypnosis. Then we were told that the first experiments would be conducted in the studio. After that the doctor would go to the other end of the building. We would hear his voice over a public address system. At that time he would show how he could hypnotize subjects over the radio.

The doctor came into the room and was introduced. He had no gimmicks or props. He looked like an average businessman. Without preliminaries he said, "For my first experiment I will count to 7 and the 10 people in the first row will be asleep . . . 1,2,3,4,5,6,7."

By the time he had finished counting those people were asleep!

What followed was amazing and bewildering, but the very first experiment tortured me. It tortured me then and for weeks after. How was it possible for an ordinary looking man to enter a room full of ordinary people and, in an ordinary voice, count to 7 and have those people in a deep sleep? I couldn't do it. You couldn't do it. What magic did this extraordinary man possess? *How did he do it?*

One day the answer came to me. He *didn't* do it. The man who introduced the doctor was the magician. He was such a salesman that he gave us such absolute confidence in the doctor's great skill with hypnotism, that we were putty in the doctor's hands.

That is the power of *confidence*. (In case you are curious, the sleep-inducing program never was produced. It worked like a magic charm, but somebody, fortunately, asked, "What about people listening to their radios while driving?" End of idea.)

Under normal circumstances, it is not an easy thing to win the confidence of people we've never met. It isn't easy, but it offers rich rewards if we make the effort.

Avoid unbelievable statements. If I were to invent a pocket television receiver that I *knew*, from constant testing, was capable of picking
up any transmission in the world, regardless of conditions, I don't
believe I would yield to the temptation to say so in my letters. Even
though it were true, I have to realize that such a statement would
challenge belief, would destroy confidence.

I'd be better off if I said, "This new television set will pick up TV
programs that the ordinary set cannot get."

People can *accept* that statement. Let them come back to me and
say, "Why, this is even better than you claimed. It can get *anything.*"
In my next letter I'll let that speak for me—a properly presented,
signed testimonial is believable.

Have you ever served on a jury? I have and I recall several
occasions when the judge, in giving the jury its instructions, said, "It
is up to you to decide which of the witnesses told the truth and which
did not. If you have good reason to believe that any of them *lied about
one thing* you have a perfect right to disregard all of the witnesses'
testimony."

When we write letters, the jury is made up of the people who read
what we write.

HOW TO BUILD CONFIDENCE

There are really two schools of thought on how to build confidence.
Patrons of one school feel that the way to build trust and faith is to pile
your claims higher and higher. Like the barber selling a bottle of hair
restorer to a completely bald man.

The man asks, "Are you sure this will grow hair on my head?"

The barber answers, "So sure that we include a comb and brush
with every bottle."

> *But the higher you pile something, the more it is
> inclined to topple over.*

The other school of thought leans on the conservative side. They feel
that keeping your claims down-to-earth—on the level—creates a
broad, firm base. Your story cannot topple over.

Those people do their confidence building by presenting all the
genuine benefits, by talking about guarantees, by emphasizing the
firm's reputation and long years of honorable trading, by use of

demonstration and sampling, and by testimonial. They also tell some of the negative features.

To illustrate the difference, let's look at two letters selling the same thing. Joe Johnson bought an assemble-it-yourself electric clock through the mail. He couldn't make it work so he sent an angry letter to the seller stating that the item arrived broken or that one or more parts were missing.

Dear Mr. Johnson,

   I have just read your letter telling me about your difficulties with our Put-It-Together-Digital Clock.

   It's a shame you've had so much trouble, but let me assure you that it is not because one or more of the parts are missing or faulty, as you suggest.

   You see, the parts used in that kit are carefully inventoried and given a thorough test before they leave here. They are made of the finest materials that money can buy. The experts who make those parts are top engineers. After all the parts are made and tested they are packed according to a tested and proven method so that nothing could possibly happen to them in transportation, no matter how roughly they are handled.

   I have seen the tests made on those packages. They pack the kit the way it will go in the mails and then take the package to the top of our 14 story building. From there they are dropped to the pavement below. After that they are placed in a furnace for twenty-four hours. After all of those tests the package is opened and the parts are tested again. That's how we know that there cannot be anything wrong with the parts.

   I suggest that you refer to the instructions once more. Read them with the greatest of care, checking each step against what you have done. I'm sure you'll find your error.

                                        Sincerely,

                                        I.M. Perfection

Now, let's try another approach.

Dear Mr. Johnson,

   I'm sorry to hear that you've had so much difficulty with the Put-It-Together-Digital Clock. I don't blame you for thinking that there may be something wrong with some of the parts, or that a part is missing. If I had gone through the same experience I would think so too.

Before you send it back to me, let me make a suggestion that may save you time and trouble.

We've shipped many of these clocks to our customers and, from time to time, some have been returned to us that proved to have defective parts. We use high grade materials and skilled people in the assembly and we have developed a mailing carton that has been very reliable in protecting the parts in shipment, but, despite all precautions, one does slip through once in a great while that is defective.

It has been our experience, however, that most of the clocks that do come back are in good working order. The customer just overlooked one step in the assembly. Frankly, when we first introduced the Put-It-Together Digital Clocks I took one home and assembled it. I did it wrong twice and felt just as you did. On the third try, however, I found my error. Everything fell into place and the clock works beautifully.

So, before repacking the clock and hauling it to the post office, I suggest that you review all the steps you've taken, checking against the instructions, just once more. Take extra care with steps 8 and 9. Those are the ones that tripped me up. If, after that, it still doesn't work, by all means return it and I'll have it double checked the moment it arrives. One way or another, you'll have a working digital clock—and quickly.

Sincerely,

I.M. Believable

Maybe I did lay it on a bit thick in that first letter, but you've all seen and heard letters and statements that came pretty close to such exaggerated unbelievable claims.

The thing I want to highlight in that second letter is the wholly believable admission that sometimes the parts are defective and that the writer sometimes makes mistakes. The claims made for the good quality and good workmanship in the material are entirely credible and the letter is calculated to make the reader like the writer. We have an extra measure of confidence in people we like.

Confidence can be built with winning logic. Richard Buck, owner of a custom kitchen firm, had been called in to plan the complete remodeling of a kitchen in a private home. He studied the situation, drew a plan, and prepared a typed estimate in which he gave the brand name of each piece of equipment he planned to install. The owners considered it for several days, and then sent Mr. Buck a letter saying they were favorably impressed but were worried about the specific equipment he had suggested. They had never heard of the brands. This was his reply

Dear Mr. and Mrs. H_____,

Your question about some of the equipment I've specified for your kitchen is a good one. You are right, I've listed at least two brands most people never heard about.

The next time we meet I'm going to show you the distributors' prices on these and on competitive well known makes. The refrigerator— freezer and the built-in oven I chose for you cost us slightly more than similar popular name units. I mention that only because I want you to know that these selections were made in order to give you the best in quality and utility, not to increase my profit.

My personal observation has been that there are two types of manufacturers in the heavy kitchen equipment field. The better known companies have huge plants, great distribution systems, and big advertising campaigns. Most retailers feature their products. What they produce is fine and many thousands of people buy and use their products and are immensely satisfied. But, in order to maintain their volume of sales year after year these big companies have to restyle constantly. They have patterned themselves after the automobile manufacturers. When the model you have looks dated, even though it is working to perfection, you become unhappy and want to change.

The other type of manufacturer is smaller and virtually unknown. The chances are his greatest volume has been in the commercial field and not in the domestic field. That is true of the two makers I have in mind for you. Both have been in business for a great number of years and have earned exceptionally good reputations. Their domestic products are sidelines and have never been promoted to the public. They cannot be excelled for quality and durability. Their products are beautifully finished. They do not become outmoded after a few years of service. You haven't seen them before and the chances are your friends haven't seen them either.

In short, I believe that the equipment I've specified for your kitchen will perform flawlessly for you for many, many years, will give you an extra measure of pride in your kitchen, and will endure and not become out-dated.

Those are the reasons why I recommended the items I did, but I am more than willing to substitute any brands you name. I hope, however, that I may have the privilege of counselling against the use of any equipment I know to be a potential source of trouble and dissatisfaction for you.

Thank you for bringing this point up so that I could give you my thinking on the subject.

Sincerely,

Richard Buck

Mr. Buck's reply combined common sense and obvious sincerity so winningly, the sale was made without any changes in specifications. He won the buyers' complete confidence with logic.

Confidence can be won with the frank admission of fault. Larry Blumenfeld, the owner of the Plymouth Printing Company, called on a printing buyer one day. The buyer was in a position to give Plymouth a great deal of work. He had given the firm two modest orders and then had stopped. The purpose of the call was to find out why.

"Frankly," the buyer said, "I couldn't tell you why, though I'll probably be in touch with you again soon."

Mr. Blumenfeld sensed that there was something more on the buyer's mind. He asked a few questions and then it came out.

The buyer explained that he had given Plymouth two jobs. Both were bulletins to go to all branches and the salespeople working out of those branches. The first had been printed in black and blue inks on white paper. The second should have been the same, but Plymouth had printed it in black ink only.

"I checked my production order to you," the buyer admitted, "and I found it was my own mistake, but had I stayed with the printer who has been doing this work for us for years he would have known better. He would have caught the error. I can't blame you and I don't and you'll hear from me soon."

When Mr. Blumenfeld returned to his office he asked for the work order on the job in question and he examined all the details carefully. The formal order, as the buyer had said, called for printing in black ink. But then he noticed, attached to it, a sample of the first job they had done for the same firm. It was stapled to the order and written across it, in the buyer's handwriting, was, "Follow for style and ink colors."

Mr. Blumenfeld wrote a letter

Dear Mr. W_____,

You shot the wrong man.

After my more than pleasant talk with you this morning I came back to the shop. For some reason I pulled out the jacket on that wayward job of yours. Yes, your purchase order said one-color, but you had also attached a copy of the former two-color job and had written on it, "Follow for style and ink colors."

I can't, for the life of me, explain why I'm happy to tell you that I am the villain in the piece and not you . . . but I am.

We don't make errors often, but we are human and we pull our share of boners from time to time. When we do we like to step up and say so and then do what we can to compensate.

The circumstances being what they are I feel we owe you something, Mr. W_____. I'd like to suggest that the next time we do one of those bulletins for you—in two colors—we will charge for a single color run with the hope that you'll consider that a fair adjustment.

> Sincerely,
>
> Lawrence Blumenfeld

The demonstration of such thorough honesty—such a sincere desire to do the right thing and to shoulder blame when it was unnecessary to do so—gave Mr. W_____ a heaping measure of confidence in Plymouth Printing. He became an important customer of the firm and has been ever since.

Making people like you breeds confidence. It blends in with so many other things we have said and will say about good letters. There's a great unanimity of feeling that stuffed shirts, ivory tower inhabitants, people with big chests and big heads, may be slightly phoney. "They sound like down-to-earth people. I feel I can trust them," is also a popular sentiment. So the more you do to make your letters reflect your personality, the more you do to make your letters friendly, warm, and demonstrative of success, the more confidence you inspire.

Where confidence exists, there is no ceiling to what can be sold by mail. A friend came to me and asked if I would help him to sell his business. He wanted to retire. We spent the better part of a day discussing the business, exploring his offices, storage, and shipping areas, and chatting with his employees. What impressed me was how clean-cut the business was. He had simplified the operation with fine intelligence. There were no problems, nothing to hide or down-play. The price he wanted seemed extremely fair.

I came to the conclusion that a letter conveying these aspects of the offer, addressed to the right audience, might be all that was needed to find a buyer.

This was the letter we used.

Ever thought of

having your own

mail order business?

A long-time friend of mine has a well established mail-order business that he is going to sell so that he can retire. It is located right here near the White Flint Shopping Mall.

Sales have been increasing each year and there is plenty of opportunity for substantial expansion. For his fiscal year ending July 31 sales exceeded $340,000. Cash flow and profit margin are excellent. Over 5,000 customers from all 50 states buy his products by mail and telephone only. 75 percent of them are repeaters. The average order is $97.50.

The items he sells are produced exclusively for him by contract manufacturers. He owns the patents, trade marks, and dies.

It is a delightfully simple business. The operation is so smooth-running and efficient that all orders are shipped within 24 hours of receipt . . . one reason why such a high percentage of his customers are repeaters.

There are no complications. My friend owns 100 percent of the stock. His realistic price includes approximately $200,000 of assets, the bulk of which is cash in the bank, clean inventory, and current receivables which he guarantees. This will be a cash transaction and the present owner will work with you for a three-to six-month transition period.

Phone or write me for further details. I'll gladly cooperate with you any way I can.

Cordially,

The mailing went to a few better than 600 carefully chosen individuals. There were 53 responses. Within a few months a mutually satisfying six-figure sale was consummated.

Did you notice that the letter attempting to make that sizeable sale wasn't even personalized?

The strength of the letter was that it accurately mirrored my friend's straightforward approach. All the essential facts were put on the table in a manner that did not challenge belief. Not a single word even hints at exaggeration. It won the confidence of the recipients.

No single letter I have ever handled has more forcefully demonstrated the limitless value of inspiring confidence. It can be assumed that the vast majority of those on the list, no matter how strongly they may have been attracted by the offer, simply were in no position to finance the purchase. Were it possible to calculate how many were in a postion to act, the percentage of response becomes astonishing.

CONFIDENCE CAN BE WON WITH AN ACCEPTABLE, REASONABLE APPROACH TO THE READER'S INTERESTS

Confidence can be won with an acceptable, low key approach to the reader's interests. The suggestion that people might put any part of their precious savings—their capital—in the hands of an institution they never dealt with before clearly has to be expressed in terms that give readers reason to feel some sense of trust. Here is how a large financial institution introduced themselves to a list of business owners and executors as a first step in getting an appointment.

Dear_____,

How much do you resent the growing demands the thoughtful management of your capital imposes on you? How much does it take away from concentration on your own specialization? These are major problems and now a century old financial company has done something about them.

Our company has developed an approach to personal capital management that is as much "today" as your morning newspaper. It is an approach worth your probing.

I would welcome the brief time it will take to tell you about the philosophy behind our personal capital management service; our readiness to accept investment accounts starting at fifty thousand dollars; how the management of your account will be tailored to your personal life-style, to your circumstances, and to your desires.

In the next day or two I will phone to ask when it will suit your convenience for me to drop by.

Cordially,

There is not a single word or statement in that letter that challenges belief. With simple directness it ties the interests and probable concerns of the readers to the potential benefits they are being asked to consider. And, since even the exposure to a discussion of this nature with a stranger is a difficult invitation to accept, the writer does not ask for action, but states that he or she will take the next step.

Another critical aspect of winning confidence in this delicate area of people's personal finances was brought to light by the results of this mailing. The letter was tested in the state where the financial institution was headquartered and in other states as well. In the home state, slightly better than 4 percent of the recipients reached by the follow-up phone call agreed to appointments. In the other states the acceptance was less than 1 percent. Clearly, the element of confidence was dramatically helped or hurt if the mailer's organization was a familiar or an unfamiliar name.

That does not mean that appointments and sales can be made economically only in the company's locality. It does mean that once the problem is recognized it must and can be solved.

Getting to know you. In this case, further testing lead to a satisfactory solution. In those regions where the institution was likely to be little known, the appointment letter became the fourth in a series of mailings.

Mailings preceding it were what might be termed "public service" letters. Each was typed on the rich, engraved stationery of the institution's president and bore his signature. As you will see from this example, they gave interesting, perhaps valuable, information and asked for nothing.

Dear_____,

I want to pass along to you an idea that may help with your cash flow, thus reducing costly borrowing.

A number of companies we deal with have departed from traditional billing practices. Instead of billing their customers at predetermined times; at the start, middle, or end of each month, they now send their invoices the day goods are shipped or services performed. The instant billing procedure has resulted in notably faster receipts and, interestingly, has sharply reduced delinquency percentages.

Throughout more than a century of close relationships with thousands of business organizations, innovative ways of handling financial matters have always been of special interest to us. When we find an idea that is particularly practical and timely I enjoy sharing the concept. I hope you find the thought in this letter to be of some value.

Sincerely,

All three letters were of this type: giving, not asking. The public service letters, mailed at erratic intervals, over a two month period, served to make the recipients feel that they knew the company and its president. By including brief mention of the institution's impressive age in one letter, its substantial assets in another, and the numbers of businesses and individuals served in the third, it succeeded in establishing a solid portrait of prestige and reliability.

Following this mental stage setting, the mailing of the letter leading to an appointment did as well, in a few cases better, than those sent to executives in the home state.

MAIN CONSIDERATIONS WHEN TRYING TO WIN THE READER'S CONFIDENCE

1. Don't try to fool the reader about anything.
2. Throw out all exaggerated claims.
3. Tell less than the whole truth if the whole truth is unbelievable.
4. Beware of innocent misstatements.
5. Bear in mind that the reader will disbelieve everything you say if you make a single misstatement.
6. Don't try overwhelming your reader with great claims.
7. Back up your claims with proof, guarantees, testimonials.
8. Write in a manner that will make the reader like you, for people are more inclined to trust those they like.
9. Use winning logic.
10. If you are wrong, say so.
11. Be straightforward, state the facts simply, and you can sell any honest proposition.
12. If confidence destroyers are revealed, a solution must be developed.

LETTERS
THAT WIN
COOPERATION

A friend told me a story that sets the stage for this subject. He was standing in front of a hotel one day waiting for a friend. While waiting, he entertained himself by watching a panhandler who was working the same side of the street. The old bum's appearance stamped him as a seasoned professional. During the few minutes my friend observed this artist at work, he saw him attempt four touches and ring the bell three times. He couldn't overhear what was being said, but he suddenly realized that he had learned an important part of this fellow's technique.

GO WITH PEOPLE—NOT AGAINST THEM

If you should ever go into the panhandling business, this might come in handy. My friend noticed that the panhandler would casually saunter up and down the street weighing each person who passed. When he found whatever it was he was looking for that stamped somebody as a hot prospect, *he would swing around and walk with him*. He never walked up and confronted a person. He always walked in the same direction.

It made a lot of sense. Had he suddenly loomed up in front of a person walking along the street, they would have to stop. They'd be annoyed. They'd side-step the obstruction and keep going. But this artist knew that. By falling in step with his client, the poor victims had little choice. They had to stroll along in company with this ragged salesman, run, or give him a handout.

No matter what you're selling, you'll sell more of it if you get in step with your prospects.

Put yourself on the other fellow's team. When a prospect or customer gets a letter from you, either of two impressions is made. You're on that person's team or you aren't. The reader won't think of it in those words, but the reaction and the results are the same.

There's no need to dwell on the advantages of making people feel you are on their side of the fence. But what is worth discussing are the ways and means of injecting that feeling.

You do it in two ways: with attitude and with words.

It isn't easy. As far as members of the public are concerned, you, the author of the letters they get, *are* the organization you represent. You're the sellers who got or are getting their money. You are the sellers and they are the buyers. People are wary of salespeople, even when they think they've made a good buy. A salesperson is stamped with self-interest. You've got to avoid that label. You must give readers reason to feel that you are interested in what is best for them.

Win cooperation with sympathy and understanding. You have to worry about other people's problems. If your thinking follows that pattern, words will creep into your letters that tell readers you are genuinely interested in them. You'll start thinking and writing in terms of "We."

We have a problem.

To take this from the vague to the exact, let's create a hypothetical case.

WINNING A CUSTOMER BACK

A subscriber cancels. Kiplinger Washington Editors, publishers of the Kiplinger Letters and Changing Times magazine, uses a very gentle approach when a long-term subscriber cancels.

Dear Mr. Smith,

I have just learned that you have asked us to cancel your Washington Letter subscription. This causes me concern because I know that you've been a client since 1972.

We don't like to lose any of our subscribers, but we especially don't like to lose a subscriber of your standing. And I am wondering if there has been some change in your situation, so that you no longer feel the Washington Letter is of value to you.

I would greatly appreciate a word from you. Meanwhile, sincere thanks for the opportunity of serving you for the past nine years.

Sincerely,

The only enclosure with this letter is a business reply envelope. Would you expect many people to be motivated to reply? Kiplinger keeps thorough records. Better than one third of the recipients of this extremely soft approach take pen in hand and answer it.

Just about 5 percent, they are advised, have passed away or left their companies, close to 10 percent have retired, another 5 percent can no longer afford to subscribe, approximately *3 percent change their minds and renew,* and some 12 percent air complaints, suggestions, and other thoughts. Editorial and sales staff members read these with interest and, not infrequently, gain valuable insight—ideas they put to work.

You work for a correspondence school. You're sitting at your desk. Everything's going along smoothly. You have only 400 letters to answer that day. And then you come to one that stops you. Here's an assignment. Less than half of it has been completed and that part is sloppy and full or errors. With it is a short note. "This stuff takes too much time. Maybe I'll find more time for the next one, but I doubt it. Herb Grove."

That isn't good, is it? Here's trouble in the offing. You look at his record and find that he still has a lot of payments to make.

There are several things you could do. You could write him a long letter telling him about the contract he's signed; that he's obligated to pay for the whole course, so he might as well make the most of it. You could. But you could do something else that might have a better result. You can get on his team.

A letter like this might do it:

Dear Mr. Grove,

How well I know how you feel. I'd be very rich if I had a dollar for every time I've said, "Wish I were twins," or, "If only each day had another eight hours."

But I had a good lesson once. I'll never forget it. My wife and I had dinner one night in the home of an old friend I hadn't seen in many years. He was a CPA and from the looks of his home he'd really struck it rich. After dinner he and I were talking. I congratulated him on how well he'd done. I said, "The CPA business must be mighty good."

He smiled and said, "I made a good investment."

I said, "Oh, the stock market."

"No," he told me, "I was studying accountancy in college. I'd been neglecting the course and I nearly got dropped. One day the Dean sent for me. He was a pretty smart apple.

I expected a bawling out. Instead he said, "How would you like to make an investment? One that will pay off at least 100 to 1, maybe much more?"

"Gee," I told him, "I sure would, but the allowance I get from home is just enough to get by on. I haven't any money."

"This doesn't have to be done today," he said, "During the next month or two, can you put yourself on a tight budget and manage to save something? It won't require too much."

"Sure I can. I will." I knew darn well that he, of all people, wouldn't give me a bad steer. This looked like a terrific opportunity.

"All right," he said, "I'll tell you what it is. Don't bother budgeting your allowance, but start right now budgeting your time. Invest it in your accountancy course and it will pay you a handsome income for the rest of your life. Every minute you invest in that course now will pay and pay and keep on paying."

My friend learned a big lesson from that and it's helped me too.

I don't know what your personal situation is, what the demands on your time are. But what that Dean said to my friend has meant so much in my own life, I thought I'd pass it on to you.

Maybe I can help you. If you think I can work with you in any way to plan your time budget, just tell me. I'd be delighted to.

Sincerely,

MAKING GOOD CUSTOMERS BETTER

Your greatest source of new business is your pool of current customers. They know your company. They know what you sell. They have demonstrated their confidence in you. When they see your company name and address on envelopes they find in their mail, they are considerably more receptive than when they see the identification of strangers.

John Nuveen & Company, the largest and oldest firm in the municipal bond business, successfully used this letter to bring existing investors an idea that can benefit investors and make them bigger customers:

Here is a way to have
more tax-free income
without investing more capital

Yes . . . you can increase the income you do not share with IRS. It
is an extra-earnings feature reserved exclusively for Nuveen Unit
Investment Trust investors.

Your present Nuveen investment is testimony to your sensitivity
to today's financial realities. You have provided yourself with
tax-free income. And because you have taken positive action to do
something about inflation, I believe that you may find great appeal
in another long step you can take in the same direction.

If you do not need your Nuveen income for current expenses, you
can sharply increase your return by compounding your tax-free
income distributions. Compounding is the reinvestment of interest
payments so that they too earn interest. Special arrangements have
been made to permit you to use those distributions, automatically,
to buy shares of the Nuveen Municipal Bond Fund . . . without
sales charge. This is the way to give yourself extra tax free earnings
without investing more capital. By doing this, your earnings are
compounded monthly. And if, at a later date, you should prefer to
receive your tax free income distributions on a regular basis once
again, your letter of instruction is all that is needed.

If this means of increasing your federally tax free earnings fits
your financial plan, just return the enclosed card. You will receive
the current prospectus of the Nuveen Municipal Bond Fund
providing more information including the management fee and
other charges and expenses. Along with it will be the form you will
use to instruct us to start you on the road to compounding your
tax-free income without investing more capital . . . adding more
power to your personal fight against inflation.

Sincerely,

Even though the letter is addressed to present clients it is not
personalized. It doesn't have to be. The caption is so inviting, because
of the potential benefit it holds forth, that it almost assures interested
readership. This is particularly true since the readers do know the
company and have evidenced their desire for tax-free income.

The entire letter capitalizes on things known about the recipients. It
emphasizes the tax-saving aspects of their offering. It reminds readers

of inflation's impact. It flatters because of the readers' demonstrated awareness and the fact that they have taken positive action.

NARRATIVE STYLE

Sure, it's a lecture, a sermon, but it has a lot of sugar coating. The narrative technique will catch readers' eyes and make them read. It's all from their viewpoint. There's no suggestion that you're worried about their money, you're just worried about them and their future.

Narrative style simplifies explanations. The narrative technique in letter writing simplifies the problem of getting on the other fellow's team. In the first place it makes your letters more interesting and more vivid. You can use it to get across a difficult point. You can use it to give an oblique lecture. No matter why or how you use it, it makes the reader like you better. Nobody likes to be bored. If your letters are entertaining, readers are more inclined to like you. Use one-upmanship on me, bore me, be too technical with me, and I am turned off. You have given me no reason to appreciate your approach or to like you. Entertain me, make yourself interesting, and you've made a friend. I like you. If I like you I am more apt to think that you like me—that you have me and my interests at heart.

Your attitude and the reader's attitude are light and fluffy things, subject to the vagaries of the lightest puffs of thought.

Narrative style brings the reader closer to you. Fiction writers know that a story is more successful if the reader can identify with your hero or heroine. Make your leading characters believable, have them act and speak in logical ways. Give them backgrounds, occupations, dreams, and thoughts that are likely to match those of your readers. When people can see themselves in stories you tell, in a favorable light, they will enjoy what they read.

The hero of the story in your letter to Mr. Grove has several things in common with him. Your story also gave the hero some elements in common with you. Among other things you and the hero were friends. While Mr. Grove is reading he begins to feel that you are *his* friend. Some of that clings when the letter ends and Mr. Grove returns to reality.

To use the narrative technique to the greatest advantage, you have to become something of a fiction writer. There will be many cases when a letter you receive presents a problem where the easiest way for you to make the writer feel a kinship with you is for you to tell a story of how you once were faced with a similar problem. You'll tell how you worked it out. Of course the solution you used is the one you hope he or she will adopt.

YOU VERSUS WE

In the early part of this chapter you read a lot about the desirability of thinking in terms of "we." It is a helpful attitude. But the *words* "we" . . . "I," "me," "my," or "our," can get you in trouble.

If you previously read a single book or heard a single talk on letter writing you are bound to have heard that the word YOU is pretty important. Someone has said that you can go through the biggest dictionary printed, from one end to the other, and you won't find a smaller word than "I," nor will you find a bigger word than "You." Another sage has pointed out that "U" comes before "I" in "B-U-S-I-N-E-S-S."

It's true. You is mighty important.

Beware of "wee-wee-itis.". Henry Hoke, one of the great pioneers of direct mail advertising, put it this way: "Avoid Wee-Wee-itis. If you fill your letters with, 'We think you should,' 'We hope you will,' 'We want you to try,' and so on . . . you've got it. You've got that fatal disease, Wee-Wee-itis."

Henry Hoke was right, but too much stress has been given to the "You versus We" business. A false impression has been created. People who read it and hear it have the notion that cramming Y-O-Us into letters is the answer. It isn't that simple.

Here's a classic example.

A big Chicago mail-order house received this letter.

Gentlemen,

Please send me the watch on page 132 of your catalogue. If it's any good, I'll send a check.

Some bright young man in the correspondence office wrote this answer:

Dear Mr. Jones,

You tell us which watch on page 132 of what catalogue and you send your check. If your check is any good, you'll get your watch.

Now there's a letter filled to the brim with YOUs. According to the books that should do the trick. There's not an I, we, me, my, mine, or our in it. One measly little "us," that's all. What it does lack, you may have noticed, is the you-attitude or you-ability. That's what counts, not the words.

The you-attitude is what counts. We're right back to that jack-in-the-box word: attitude. Forget the word "You" and remember the you-attitude. And the you-attitude can be defined by saying, it's the answer to the question everybody asks when reading any business letter, "What's in it for me?"

You-attitude is writing the letter from the other person's point of-view.

That poses a problem for some people when they write a letter that attempts to sell something. The motive is selfish. They can't divorce their minds from the fact that they want to get something from the person to whom they're writing.

Suppose you were in the business of selling mechanical action display units for retailers to use in their store windows. A letter comes to you from the owner of a large stationery store. The writer wants information on one of the units you make. You want to complete a sale, of course. You'll send your illustrative literature and prices, and you write a covering letter to go with those items. Your letter can do either of two things. It can show that you are eager to make a sale and a profit for yourself, or it can show that you are eager to help this store owner to make more sales and profits. Here's how you might do the latter.

Dear Ms. Gaines,

You have an unusually good opportunity to get maximum values from the Tell-All Display you inquired about. Thanks for asking and for giving me the opportunity to show you how you can capitalize on this positive attention winner.

You are in a business that deals with thousands of types of merchandise. Every time you plan a window display you must have an immensely complex decision to make. Your windows will hold just so many items. The more you try to jam into the windows the less attention you can focus on the item or items you are most anxious to feature. The more you put into the windows, the more danger there is of creating a hodgepodge where nothing stands out.

That's why the Tell-All is so important to you.

When you get your Tell-All, try an experiment. If you have been in the habit of putting 30 or 40 items in your window, cut it down to six or eight of your best traffic pullers. The Tell-All will sell your other departments.

You can put as many as 50 items on the Tell-All in the space you formerly used to display just five or six items. The Tell-All will carry illustrations in addition to headlines and prices. Because it moves, it attracts.

Be sure to keep your Tell-All about three feet back from the window itself. If it is closer than that only a limited number of people can watch it at one time. Put it back a few feet and dozens can watch . . . and they will.

With this letter you'll find illustrations of the Tell-All and the full story of how you will put this great merchandiser to work. The prices are there too. Your Tell-All unit will be shipped at once and will be working for you just as quickly as you prepare your copy for it. The literature shows you how easy it is to prepare the copy.

Thanks again for asking. If you want any additional information, by all means let us help you in every way we can. You'll find the answers to nearly every question in the literature and you'll also find an addressed and postage-paid reply form you can use now to order your Tell-All for immediate shipment.

Sincerely,

The score: 1 Me, 1 Us, 1 We, dozens of You, but the major factor is that there is a you-attitude throughout.

Seeing People. An old story illustrates the point. There was a man who lived in a comparatively small community. He was a businessman and had made a huge fortune. He'd made it the hard way, hard on everybody he met. He'd gotten along in years and as age came on he lost some of his drive. Loneliness took its place. He had no friends or family. His life was empty and he began to feel ill.

He went to his doctor to see what was wrong. The doctor knew his patient pretty well.

The doctor said, "Go over to the window and tell me what you see."

The old man, puzzled, got up, went to the window and looked out at he busy street below. "I see people," he said.

"All right," the doctor said, "Now walk across the room and look at that mirror and tell me what you see."

The old fellow shrugged his shoulders and went over to the mirror.

"What do you see?" the doctor prompted.

"I see myself, of course."

"Ah," the doctor cried, "There's your trouble. Both are pieces of glass, but as soon as one is smeared with silver you can't see anybody but yourself.''

Look out of windows when you write. Letters that are written by people who are looking out of windows, rather than into mirrors, have the you-attitude. And when you have the you-attitude, there generally aren't too many first person pronouns present.

I've spent a number of years conducting a course in business letter writing at the American University in Washington, D.C. Of course we talk about this subject. Still, when checking over the class's assignments I've found that they average 17 first person pronouns per page in the early part of the course. Later I get tough and tell them that 4 is par for the course. I don't practice it to that extent myself, but it is good training.

The greatest difficulty people seem to have, in cutting down on their wee-wee-itis, is in terms of describing what they are offering. They'll make statements like, ''I'm sure that when I come to see you, I can bring to your attention some of the fine merchandise we have been satisfying our clients with for many years.'' That has five first persons in one sentence; one more than is permitted for the entire letter.

Most first person references are needless. The ''I'm sure,'' is completely unnecessary. It does no selling at all.

The rest could be switched to, ''When you make this appointment, you'll see some of the wonderful merchandise that has been pleasing our clients for years.'' That leaves 1, and all the emphasis is on the you's, which is as it should be.

Another wrong notion, the editorial ''we'' may be all right in editorials, but it has crept into letter writing where it seldom is right. A letter is, or should be, a very warm, personal document, an exchange between two people: individuals. Many letter writers have the strange idea that saying ''We'' instead of ''I'' is modest and creates a good impression.

The impression it actually creates is that the reader has received a communication from a company, a corporation, an institution, a board of directors. They can't sense an individual. And if they can't, all of the valuable human relationships that can do so much to create a good feeling are lost.

Using the word ''I'' expresses personal interest.

Using the word ''We'' expresses a job being done for a company.

You win cooperation by demonstrating your genuine interest in the people you write to, by showing that your primary interest is to serve the person reading your letter.

In many cases it makes good sense to blend the "we" and the "I" in a letter. You can say, for example, "I will see to it that we will handle your billing in the manner you requested." That adds up because you alone will see to it, not a committee, but the company does the billing. You don't.

The you-attitude in a job application. Putting the emphasis on you in a letter applying for a job has proven a problem for many people. They ask, "How can I apply for a job without devoting most of the letter to talk about myself?"

That seems like a well-founded question until you give it some thought. Surely, the potential employer who reads such a letter is asking, more than most people, "What's in it for me?"

Too many writers of letters seeking employment become so absorbed in themselves and what they want, they disregard what the potential employer may want. Here's a letter of application that puts the stress on the reader rather than the writer.

Dear Ms. G _____,

You are looking for a personnel director for your Chicago office. My background and qualifications may give you what you are seeking.

With this letter you'll find a detailed resume, but highlighting a few points in this letter may prove helpful.

You'll have dozens of applications that can match and exceed mine for scholastic achievement. But I've always admired your company and its dynamic, unique concepts. I have studied it and have adopted a vast number of your excellent departures in the personnel realm.

The background and experience you'll be getting if I am chosen is almost the equal of putting someone in that job who has grown up in your own organization.

Yours is the organization I believe I can do the most for and, therefore, the one I'll be happiest with. At your convenience I'll come to your office for a personal interview. Just say when.

Sincerely,

Admittedly, it isn't always possible to link yourself to a company as forcefully as this applicant did. Before writing any letter of application, however, it will pay you to learn all you can about the prospective employer. Use what you learn to talk in terms of that organization's interests and how your experience can best serve those interests.

GETTING THE ANSWER OR ACTION YOU WANT

All who buy goods and services, for business or personal use, occasionally have reason to write letters asking for help or adjustment, only to get no answer at all, or completely inadaquate responses. Undoubtedly, you have had such experiences. After two or three efforts you picture your letters going into the trash without being opened, or turned over to an inflexibly programmed computer.

These are frustrating experiences, but in many cases your problem can be resolved by going right to the top, the president of the company or some other highly placed executive. Your public library carries various directories that will give you the names of the principal executives of thousands of companies. But, even if you don't have the name of the president you can address your letter properly by using the title. The chances are good that you'll get to the right person. If enough is involved, invest in a phone call to get the name you want and the correct spelling.

Don't use your letter to attack. You may be seething with justified anger, but you must decide if you want to make yourself feel better by letting off steam, or if you want to get an answer or action. If it is the latter, supress your irritation and put yourself in the president's shoes. Write your letter in a manner calculated to win total cooperation.

Margaret Mason bought a watch by mail. After two years it stopped running. She sent the watch back with a covering letter. She never got an answer. After months of fruitless effort to get some response, she dug up the name of the company's president and wrote this letter.

Dear Mr. Wade,

   This letter can prove to be helpful to both of us. As the busy head of your company you probably are not aware of my problem. I feel equally certain that you cherish the reputation of your company and place a high value on the good will of your customers.

   Almost ten months ago I returned a digital watch I had bought from you. It needed repairs. In my accompanying letter I said that the guarantee had expired; to please let me know what the repair charges would be and I would send a check by return mail. That letter and three others that followed have never been answered. A claim was filed with the post office on the insured package, but they now inform me that the package was received and signed for by one of your employees, a photo copy of that signed postal receipt is enclosed. I still have had no word from your company, nor do I have a watch.

All of this must come as upsetting news to you, but knowing the facts gives you the opportunity of making certain that such practices will be stopped and steps will be taken to deal with your customers in a considerably better way. I will appreciate your looking into this situation and letting me know what can and will be done to get the watch back to me, repaired or unrepaired.

Sincerely,

Mr. Wade's prompt response said:

Dear Mrs. Mason,

You have done me a great favor and I'm happy to tell you that a new watch is on its way to you. There will, of course, be no charge. It is the least I can do to try to make amends for the unpardonable manner in which you have been treated.

Mr. Wade's letter went on to give a detailed explanation of why his employees had fouled up the deal and the steps being taken to be sure that such negligence would not happen again. The point is that her letter, because of its cooperative attitude, won Mr. Wade's cooperation. Mrs. Mason got what she wanted.

MAIN CONSIDERATIONS WHEN YOU SEEK TO WIN COOPERATION

1. Show readers you are on their teams, that you want to help.
2. Worry about the other person's problem, and let that concern come through in your letters.
3. The narrative style helps to put your attitude across.
4. The narrative style brings the reader closer to you.
5. Emphasize the "you" and play down the "we."
6. Adopt a "you-attitude."

7. See people when you are writing.

8. Avoid needless first person expressions.

9. The editorial ''we'' doesn't belong in letters.

10. Put aside anger if you want cooperation.

TELL THE READER
WHAT YOU WANT

Just what do you have in mind? If you are going to take the time and trouble to write a business letter, you must have *some* goal in mind.

The last time you heard a political speech the chances are you recall that the speaker ended up by claxoning, "So vote for my candidate, Rodney Runner!"

The next time you turn on your television set keep an eye on commercial announcers. They'll spend a good part of their time telling you how wonderful their product is and they'll end up by saying, "So rush now to your nearest drug store and ask for Lollipop Lipstick!"

And when somebody comes to your home or office and tries to interest you in their proposition, just watch. At the *end* of the presentation you'll be asked if you'll buy.

When you write letters, it will pay you to follow those examples.

Everything is prelude to the closing paragraph. There are two reasons for this. First, it simply isn't logical to ask people to do something until you've told them what and why. Secondly—and this is particularly true in letter writing—you can't afford to devote your letter to the what and the why expecting readers to decide how and when to take the action you want them to take.

KEEP YOUR EYES ON THE GOAL

In most business letters, there is a purpose to be achieved. You want the reader to do something. You want some specific action taken. You want to start the reader going in a given direction. Seldom do you write a letter without the thought of achieving something by what you have written. If it's a five paragraph letter, the first four should describe and elaborate, but the final paragraph calls for the name on the line, the ring of the cash register, the check in the mail, the assignment carried out.

Nor do these objectives make your letters selfish affairs. If your letters reflects the right mental attitude, they lead readers to action that will be beneficial to them.

What's said last is first remembered. When you finish your dinner, what flavor clings to your taste buds? The sweetness of the dessert. That was the last thing you had and, therefore the first thing you recall. When you write a letter the most vivid impression retained, if your letter is well planned, is the final call for action.

Assume that you are writing to Charlene Prospect encouraging her to buy something she inquired about. The whole purpose of your letter is to get her excited, to sell her on the benefits, to induce her to take action.

What does that take?

HERE'S A FORMULA
−PICTURE, PROMISE, PROVE, AND PUSH

You start your letter with a commanding statement that makes prospects want to read what follows. You paint some mental pictures of the things your product can do for them. Next you link that dream to your specific product or service. You promise that this is the way their dream can come true. You back up that statement by offering proof: testimonials, case histories, and specific facts about your product or service. You end up by pushing for action, spelling out what they should and must do right now if they're to have all that pleasure or profit.

Many letter writers leave out the *Push*. They draw a handsome picture. They make fine promises. They support the promises with solid proof, and then run for the bus without kissing their date goodnight.

Never forget that people are lazy. They do not take the thoughts sprinkled throughout your letter and translate them to personal action. They may read every word, they may nod in agreement, but they still put the letter aside and get back to making their selections for the office football pool.

Ask for the order. A good letter writer is a good translator. A good letter writer puts the products on the counter, one by one, and then, having given all of the sales points and benefits, brings it all together, summarizes the features, and the benefits and asks for the order. And if the writer fails to ask for the order, it all amounts to a page full of pointless conversation and nothing more. The writer has gained nothing. The reader has gained nothing.

Make it easy to act. You must do more than ask for the order. You must point out what they will lose by not agreeing. You must show why it is to their advantage to agree immediately, and then you must make it as easy as possible for them to take positive action.

Put all those factors into the last paragraph of each letter you write.

You can't afford to wait for the last paragraph to let readers know what you want them to do. The sooner you tell them the better. But it does pay—it is essential—that the final paragraph be devoted to that subject *exclusively*.

ASK YOURSELF, "WHAT ACTION DO I WANT?"

An excellent question to ask yourself before you start any letter is, "What is this letter intended to accomplish?"

Keep the answer foremost in your mind. You'll automatically end up with the right kind of a last paragraph and a letter that builds up to a fitting climax.

There are many professional letter writers who carry that idea out to what might be considered an extreme. They write the final, action-demanding paragraph first. Then they go back and write the balance of the letter.

It is a sound idea. It gives your letter purpose and cohesion. You'll find, if you should try this technique, that the rest of the letter practically writes itself.

Failure to ask for action is a common weakness. At one time I conducted a series of courses in salesmanship at The American University in Washington, D.C. Half of the 16 week course was devoted to "Closing the Sale." A great deal of time was spent establishing the need for a salesperson to be a strong closer. Then we'd explore the reasons why most salespeople shy away from the crucial point in the sale: a weakness present in far too many salespeople and letter writers. Having established our foundation, we would go into the various techniques that may be used to close a sale.

If you want people to accept your product, your service or your ideas, you are selling. Many of the techniques that are used by salespeople can be applied to your letter-writing.

Of course they will buy. One highly useful closing technique is based on your revealing a firm belief that your customers will buy. Everything you say demonstrates your conviction that your proposals will be accepted. Not a single "if" will appear in your letters. Certainty is contagious.

In your closing paragraph you don't ask whether the reader will buy. Instead you ask, "How many?" . . . "What color?" . . . "What method of shipment?" . . . "How do you prefer to pay?"

People are lazy. Making a decision calls for mental effort. Making a decision creates a great inner struggle. It is unpleasant and difficult. People appreciate the professional salesperson who eases them into *good* decisions. Showing a total absence of doubt in your mind helps remove the doubts in the customer's mind.

Can a letter be that positive? It surely can be.

Dear Mr. Boller,

In your April 8th letter you asked for the current price on 14 of the Model L-42. The price, delivered to your showroom, Mr. Boller, is $874.33, which includes all taxes.

It's fortunate that you asked at this time because some immensely worthwhile improvements have just been made on the Model. They'll move faster for you, and you'll probably be the first in your area with the new ones.

Mr. Boller, we can ship to you by truck or express. Trucking will take about three extra days, but we'll save about $20 in crating costs which will be passed along to you. It will be deducted from the quoted price.

As soon as this letter reaches you, phone me collect telling me which mode of shipment you want and shipment will be made immediately.

Gratefully,

There's no question asked in this letter as to whether or not Mr. Boller will buy. The writer assumes he'll buy and simply asks him how to handle the delivery. The final paragraph offers a direct and easy way to take the desired action. The same attitude makes this next letter a strong closer, and the writer used another technique to make it easy for the customer to act.

Dear Ms. Sollar,

We are getting close to that time of the year when you customarily place your order for our stuffed animals so that you are ready for your Easter Business. For the last two years you have ordered:

1 gross of chicks, item 9072

3 dozen panda bears, item 6554

3 dozen teddy bears, item 886

2 dozen rabbits, item 06643

You told me that the rabbits went unusually well last year. Do you want to increase that, or any other of the items I've listed? You'll find a copy of this letter enclosed, along with a stamped and addressed envelope. Use them to O.K. or to amend the quantities you want. Drop it in the mail now and as soon as it reaches me your merchandise will be on its way.

Have a great Easter season!

Cordially,

Use an "Off-target" close. Another successful technique is also based on your understanding of the difficulties people face when fighting the battle of indecision.

A number of years ago the Cadillac Company learned of one salesman in Long Island, New York, who had an amazing number of sales to his record. This was during a period when high-priced cars were hard to sell. They sent a big shot from the national sales department to observe this man in action. At first it looked as though he was doing the exact job every other Cadillac salesperson was doing. He'd show people all the features of the car, point out the new gadgets, have them sit behind the wheel, and he'd answer their questions. But at that point when the average salesperson would ask if they would like to buy a Cadillac, this man did something different. He took from his pocket a little folder. The folder showed various styles of lettering available for a plate with the owner's name to go on the dashboard.

"Which do you prefer," he'd ask, "the block letter or the script for your personal plate?"

And when the customer named their choice they actually, and with their eyes wide open, were saying, "Yes, I'll buy a Cadillac."

There's really nothing amazing about that. The salesman understood people. No matter how much shoppers may want something, if a big sum of money is involved, it isn't easy for them to overcome all the negatives pouring into their minds. It is the struggle for decision. This salesman sugar-coated the pill by asking for ridiculously small, off-target decisions.

There are many ways to use the off-target technique. A woman had her six year old son downtown with her and found she'd left her wallet home. She had no carfare and they lived quite a few miles away. She realized that such a long walk would exhaust the boy, would make him irritable and unhappy.

She solved the problem by saying to her son, "Dicky, there's a wonderful toy store just five blocks up this street. I've always wanted to show you their windows." After they had seen the toys she thought of something else Dicky would like to see, pigeons in a little park. Thus, stage by stage, they moved uptown. When they got home Dicky's legs were tired, but he was exhilarated and happy. He'd had a wonderful time.

Keep this technique in mind when you are writing a letter asking someone to do a big job. Thrust it at them in one big, frightening package and they may resist. Present it as a series of easy steps and you have a far better chance of winning agreement.

You are advertising manager of the Williams Weatherproofing Materials Company. You sell your materials to local weatherproofers. You have just decided on a national advertising program that calls for a lot of cooperation on the part of the companies that handle your products.

Each of your customers will have to get advertising display rates from all of their local papers and send them to you. You will then tell them what papers they should use and what size ads. They have to design their own ads so that the advertising will tie in with their individual methods of operation, but since you are going to foot the bill, you want to approve the ads they create. The day the ads appear you want them to send you tear sheets so that you know you are being billed for the proper amounts. You also want to make offset copies of their ad and mail them to their customers and prospects. Experience has shown that you can't depend on them to do this, so, to be sure it is done you will do it yourself. You therefore have to ask them to compile and send you a mailing list. You're asking them to do many things. This is the letter:

Dear Ms. Moogan,

To help you to increase your sales this fall we're going to spend some money in your community to tell the public what you have to offer.

You'll undoubtedly agree that the plan is unusual. Instead of sending you some mats that talk about our products, we prefer that you advertise your own business and your own methods of operation. Devote just 25 percent of the ad to Williams products and we'll pay the full cost. That is a departure, isn't it?

To get the ball rolling just ask your local papers to send you their rate cards and then shoot them to me. Once we see the rates we'll tell you what size ads to plan for which papers.

When we okay the ads you plan to run, our advertising people will cooperate with you, if you wish. They will offer some helpful suggestions for layout and copy.

But that isn't all. This gravy train is a long one, carrying a big payload.

The day the ads appear, air mail tear sheets to us. The accounting department will check them out so that we can send you a check and enough copies of your own ad will be printed and mailed to all of your customers and prospects entirely at our expense.

Does putting all those copies in the mail sound like a big job for you: It would be, but we're going to do it for you. All you do is send us the list. We'll do the rest and you don't pay a dime for the whole campaign.

Let's get an early start so that there will be no last minute problems or delays. Now before you put this letter aside please phone the local papers to request the rate cards. I'll be grateful if you'll be sure they reach me before the end of next week.

My warmest regards.

Cordially,

Even though Ms. Moogan had been told of every job she'll be expected to do, it boils down to a few phone calls now. The rest will come in easy stages. The task does not look like a big one and the rewards have been made to look big.

TELL HOW AND TELL WHEN

In direct mail selling it has been found that the last paragraph of a sales letter must do more than ask for action. It must spell out exactly what the reader should do to take such action. For example, if a reply card is enclosed it is best to say, ". . . so all you have to do is put your name, address, and the color you want on the enclosed postage-paid, addressed card. Drop it in the mail today,'' or words to that effect.

It is important that you spell out all that detail because test after test has shown that if you fail to tell them that there *is* a card, results will drop. That isn't because people are stupid. It's because the impulse to take the requested action hangs by a slender, delicate thread. You cannot afford to add one bit of weight to the request hanging on the end of that thread.

Make it *easy* for them to do what you want them to do. Take nothing for granted. Don't force them to translate suggestions to specific action. S-p-e-l-l i-t o-u-t.

Telling your reader to take action *now* is particularly important. How many times have you received a piece of direct mail that interested you and then you put the reply aside till you had more time?

A few days later you came across it and said, ''What's this doing here?'' *Bong!* Into the wastebasket. All the emotional reaction to the letter was gone, dissipated, watered down by everything else that happened since you first read the letter. The impulse to take action was gone.

Explain the need for speed. Use all the ingenuity at your command to give them reasons why it will pay them to take the desired action at once. Perhaps a shortage is on the horizon. Maybe prices are going to go up. Those are splendid reasons if they are true. If they are not true leave them alone. Find some other reasons.

If you have no dramatic, logical appeals for immediate action, you can rely on the fact that most people know their own weaknesses.

Try closing your letter with this thought: ''You can see the many benefits you'll gain from this suggestion, Mr. Bennett. Now, while you have all the facts, before the pressure of other important matters diverts your thoughts, please call your plant superintendent and ask him or her to send me the specifications right away. I'll rush the plans and estimates right back to you.''

That closing presents an acceptable reason why Mr. Bennett should call for his superintendent at once. It also injects an added element to the feeling of the need for speed. The promise to ''rush'' the plans and estimates will have its influence on the reader.

Instead of telling them what to do, tell what you will do. Several of the letters you have read used the strategy of telling the reader what the writer will do next. It is a very effective technique. Not only does it eliminate the need for you to simply *hope* that people will do as you ask, it usually puts the recipient in a desirable frame of mind. For example:

Dear_____,

It would be interesting and disturbing if you kept a record of the hours you spend managing the assets you have accumulated. Those are hours you could use profitably pursuing your own profession.

Many successful professional and business leaders share that problem with you. This is one of the primary reasons why our organization now uses its better than a century of financial experience to bring individual asset management to people with investments amounting to $50,000 or more.

You will be fascinated with the freshness of the approach we have taken and the way in which even your lifestyle is given serious consideration by your money manager.

In the next day or so I will phone so that we can choose a mutually convenient date for me to come by to tell you the full story.

Cordially,

A provocative story has been told. It is a story that deals with a subject that most business and professional people take very seriously. They worry about how to handle their assets in a chaotic economy, and they worry about needless drains on their valuable time. The writer is talking their language. At the same time the writer is a stranger. Under normal circumstances there will be a high degree of reluctance to respond to the suggestion of a face-to-face meeting. But that decision does not have to be made. Nobody is asking the reader to return a card, sign anything, or to make a phone call. The writer is going to call.

Knowing that the writer will call motivates the reader to give some genuine thought to the subject covered by the letter. Nobody enjoys appearing uninformed, at a loss for words. Pride alone dictates the desire to be prepared for the phone call. The thought process involved may lead to the conclusion that when the call is received, it can do no real harm to make an appointment. On the other hand the decision might be to stoutly rebuff any arguments as to why the appointment shoud be made.

And then—surprise—the call comes through and the representative of the big financial insitutition doesn't advance a single sales point. Here is all that is said:

"This is so-and-so of Big Financial Institution, Mr. _____.
You just had a letter from me. When is a convenient day and time for me
to come to your office? Would a week from Thursday fit your schedule,
or would you prefer to make it Wednesday of that week?"

It is much easier to elect one of the suggested dates than it is to make
a statement that refuses any meeting. Testing and experience have
established that this combination of a letter saying you will phone,
followed within two or three days, by the simple phone conversation
quoted, will get an affirmative response from one-third of the people
called.

THINGS TO REMEMBER WHEN ENDING YOUR LETTER

1. Every business letter attempts to accomplish *something*.
2. Your final paragraph is read last and remembered longest.
3. Devote the entire final paragraph to your request for action.
4. Have that final request for action clearly in mind throughout the letter.
5. When asking for action, summarize all the reasons why.
6. Spell out *what* you want done.
7. Spell out *how* to do it.
8. Use the proven closing techniques of personal selling.
9. Show why it is important to take action now.
10. Place the action on your own shoulders.

HOW TO HANDLE RESPONSES TO ADVERTISING

One of the greatest mysteries in the conduct of big business today is the astonishing lack of skill and organization in the handling of inquiries inspired and invited by advertising. Here is one of the greatest blind spots in the advertising picture.

Flip the pages of any national magazine. You'll see page after page of costly ads, many in full color, inviting you to use the handy coupon at the foot of the ad. The reader fills out and mails the coupon requesting a free, beautifully illustrated booklet on *How to Chew Tobacco Like a Professional*. And then: the long, long wait.

SPEED IS THE MOST IMPORTANT ELEMENT

Let's scalp typical coupon clippers and look inside their minds.

Tearing out a coupon, finding a pen that works and squeezing the required information into the limited space offered, finding an envelope, searching the ad for the proper address and putting that on the envelope, digging under last month's bills in search of a stamp, and then walking to the mail box all take time and effort.

To most people, that's a lot of work. It takes a great deal of motivation to coax the average person to put forth so much effort.

The ad has to be unusually compelling. It has to set fire to the reader's imagination. And that's exactly what it does.

You have to reach coupon-senders while the fire is burning. Strike a match and hold it straight up. See what happens. It starts out with a bright, hot glow. With each second that passes the flame grows smaller and weaker. Very rapidly the flame dies down to just a small ember and then it goes out. Nothing is left but a cold, dead ash.

People who mail coupons are just like a match. They've been inflamed by your ad. In the bright glow of their enthusiasm they take all the steps needed to mail the coupon. As the days go by, without response, the flame grows weaker. It is dampened and subdued by a myriad of other influences and distractions and by the icy water of being ignored.

The sooner your advertised offer reaches your coupon clipper, the greater the chance that the flames of interest are still burning. The longer you take the greater the chance that their interest, like the match, has become a cold dead ash. You've lost all the priceless value of their original enthusiasm.

While preparing material for this book, I arranged to have responses mailed to nearly 1,200 national advertisers. Whenever and wherever an ad appeared offering a booklet, a sample, information, or anything else, the invitation was accepted. A coupon was clipped, a postcard, or a letter was mailed.

The ads responded to, for the most part, were handsomely designed, well written, and run on the costly pages of national magazines and major newspapers. *Nearly two-thirds of the replies we sent in response to those costly allurements, were completely ignored; nothing ever happened.*

Those who did reply to the inquiries took an average of 45 days to get around to it.

Fewer than 5 percent of those who did reply ever follow-up: *wanton, asinine, needless waste of untold millions of dollars.*

Intelligent, profitable advertising of this type demands four steps, and all four must be completed and in place before the public sees anything.

Step 1. The ad itself . . . the invitation to send for a something.

Step 2. Total preparation for the immediate handling of all inquiries. What is the projection? On the basis of past experience (if not your own, the experience of others and the assumptions of experienced, knowledgeable specialists) how many inquiries are anticipated? Is the "response package" to be sent to all who inquire now planned, written, designed, printed, assembled, and as ready as it can be for the addressing and any planned personalization so that it can be on its way as quickly as possible?

Is there sufficient personnel on the job and trained to take the measures required to move the response packages out promptly and accurately? Is the equipment needed in place, checked out, and ready? Have you anticipated questions the public may ask and have thoughtfully prepared answers been processed to handle them: Are the mechanics for supplying the anticipated questions, and those that have not been anticipated, planned and ready?

Step 3. Does everybody in your organization know what your advertising is saying? Have they been told why it is being said? Do they appreciate the degree of responsibility they carry to support what is being said? Do they realize that they can severely damage the increased business and heightened good will you are trying to develop if they fail to fulfill their roles fully and properly? Do they know how much they can add to the good this campaign can accomplish if they measure up to the image being created?

Have you taken the time and trouble to give everyone the vital knowledge that each of them is important, that their wholehearted involvement, whether it involves the writing of letters, handling phone calls, filling or delivering orders, adjusting errors, billing, production—anything—will help the company to grow, will help each of them to grow?

Step 4. Have the follow-up mailings been planned, written, designed, printed, scheduled, and are they all in place and ready to go?

Not a single one of the four steps is more important than the others. Until all four are completely ready it is wasteful and pointless to advertise.

Answer all inquiries within 24 hours. Before you do any advertising that invites inquiries, set up the mechanics of responding to the inquiries you receive so that they can be handled within 24 hours. Reach the people who inquire while the flame is still burning brightly.

Tell them you've hurried to reply. Replying within twenty-four hours is good business and it always pays to capitalize on good business. Tell them that you hurried to respond to give them what they requested.

A national life insurance company uses the mails to offer their policies. Their mailed offer tells readers that if they will fill out a brief reply form they will be given the exact rates that apply to them without charge of obligation. The company responds to such inquiries the day they arrive. This is the letter they mail.

Here are the facts

you asked for . . .

The moment we had your card asking for the exact rates on the Juvenile Capital Accumulator policy we hurried to the files, figured them for you and here they are . . .

Based on the present age of your child the rate is $13.46 per quarter for each $1,000 unit.

Thanks for asking.

The reasons we hurried are because we appreciate the interest you have shown and because time is such a vital factor in insurance. Time is so important because none of us can foresee what unexpected events may occur today or tomorrow . . . because rates go up as the child's age increases . . . because the sooner you start your Juvenile Capital Accumulator policy working for the future welfare of your child the more it can accomplish for you.

For your benefit, here is a review of the features of this unusual policy:

1. Each $1,000 unit jumps to a $5,000 unit on the child's 21st birthday with no increase in premium.
2. The policy remains in force for the child's entire life, but it becomes a paid-up policy—no more premiums to be paid—after age 65.
3. Because cash values in this policy build up rapidly you have important cash reserves to draw on when the heavy expenses of college education, the start of a business, the building of a home, etc., must be met.
4. You can have as many $3,000 units as you desire.

And because time is so important, I urge you to fill out the enclosed application now and hurry it back to us in the addressed and postage-paid envelope you'll find with this letter. Your policy will go in force at once.

Cordially,

In this letter the element of speed of reply is used throughout, setting the pace for the reader.

ALWAYS USE A COVERING LETTER

Test after test in mass mailings has proven that a covering letter is immeasurably important when you mail literature. Sales frequently have doubled when a covering letter went in the envelope with literature as compared with the literature riding alone. The reason is clear.

One of the greatest forces in each of us is the desire to be appreciated. A folder or booklet, no matter how handsomely designed and printed, says to the reader, "I'm for the masses." Clearly, it has been produced in volume for anybody and everybody.

A letter, however, is a personal document from one person to another. The prospect took the time and trouble to write to you. Common courtesy demands that you respond. Stuffing a printed folder into an envelope is an incomplete response.

FORM LETTERS CAN SEEM PERSONAL

The covering letter does not have to be individually typed. It doesn't have to carry the name and address of the recipient. It should be on a letterhead. It should be in typewriter type. It should have a printed reproduction of a handwritten signature, preferably in a colored ink. In place of the customary salutation, use a caption that adds to the personal quality of the letter.

A form letter that shakes hands with your customers. Here is a form letter mailed to those who inquired about a weekly newsletter on foreign exchange produced by International Reports of New York City:

Here is the booklet

you requested

Your interest in International Reports is sincerely appreciated.

The folder you requested, which is enclosed with this letter, gives you the details of the weekly service. You'll find that it also tells you how each issue is written and how our network of nearly one hundred correspondents, scattered all over the globe, cable their reports to our editors each week.

You'll see, as you read the folder, how the authoritative news that will be on your desk every Monday morning can guide you to extra profits or help you to avoid serious losses in your transactions involving foreign exchange.

After you've read the details and have seen what this weekly flow of information can accomplish for you, please accept this warm invitation to take a no-risk subscription. The booklet will show you how you can actually receive and read enough issues of International Reports to learn for yourself how importantly it can help you, without risk or obligation.

At the back of the booklet you'll find the no-risk subscription form and an addressed envelope. Mail them today.

Thanks again for your interest.

Cordially,

Guenter Reimann, Editor

The letter should sell the literature. Notice how the *International Reports* letter not only creates the feeling of being a very personal message, it accomplishes another important function.

It gives the reader added incentive to read the literature thoroughly. No matter how fast the inquiry was answered, the original flame of interest in bound to have died down to some extent. The letter makes the flame higher, brings it back to its original intesity.

The effective letter calls for action. Calling for action is another job the covering letter should handle. It tells readers that their purpose in studying the accompanying litterature is to reach a decision and to take action. You can't afford to leave that thought to the readers.

The sooner, the more often, and the more firmly you plant the action thought in the readers' minds, the better your chances of getting the action you want.

YOUR COVERING LETTER SETS THE STAGE

The next time you watch a stage show, attend a night club performance, or watch a show of the variety type on television, you can learn an important lesson about letter writing. There is always a star act, a featured performer. Watch.

The house lights are dimmed. The drums roll. The trumpets blare. A bright spotlight is thrown on the stage. The curtains part with sudden drama and . . . *there is the star.*

What does that do to the audience? It says, it shouts, "This is important. This is great. This is the big moment you've been waiting for."

You inch forward on your seat, eager, full of excited anticipation. You have been lured into full attention. Your undistracted acceptance of what is to follow has been raised to the highest level of appreciation.

ROLL THE DRUMS FOR YOUR LITERATURE

Steal a page from the professional showman's book. The covering letter you send with your selling literature will do more for you if you, like the showman, use your skills to make readers eager and excited about the material they are about to read.

Your covering letter introduces the literature. Your covering letter performs the function of the program chairperson of your club who gets up and introduces the guest speaker. If your chairperson does the job well you have been sold on the reasons why it will pay you to give the speaker your faith and your full attention.

Your covering letter should plant the mental seed of the need for action, the importance of making an affirmative decision, and doing it now.

Notice, in the following letter, how the writer first reinforced the recipient's interest in the subject, presold the accompanying, requested, literature, and then stressed the advantage of immediate action and reminded the prospect of what might be lost by failing to act promptly. In addition, in case the reader might hold back because of lack of total understanding or lingering doubts, the door was held open by the suggestion that a toll-free phone call would be welcomed.

You are right . . .

When you replied to our ad you made the decision that now is that proper time to plan for your retirement years. You are right. It is one type of planning that increases in difficulty with each passing year. Now is the most advantageous time for you to take action.

In this folio is everything you need to see what the Keogh Plan's tax shelter can do for you—how to organize your plan in a way that suits you, your needs and your thinking—the steps to take to get your accumulation of dollars for retirement started at once.

If we have failed to make everything clear, or if there are any questions you or your advisor would like to ask please accept this invitation to make a toll-free phone call. We will do everything we can to be helpful.

If all of the benefits are clear—if what you can lose by postponing the start of your plan is evident—there never will be a better time to start than this day. Put your check and application in the mail now.

Cordially,

NRI is one of the country's bigger and more successful correspondence schools. Their ads appear in many national magazines, inviting prospective students to fill in and mail the coupon that will bring them a free booklet describing the courses they have to offer.

Your letter sharpens the reader's appetite for the enclosure. Here's the covering letter that goes out with requested booklets detailing the facts about their course on Servicing Electrical Appliances.

Dear Friend:

Your inquiry arrived today, and here is your copy of the booklet, "How to Learn Servicing Electrical Appliances."

[Even though the prospect's name is not typed on the letter, "Your inquiry arrived today," makes the reply very personal.]

"How to Learn Servicing Electrical Appliances" will tell you exactly what is covered in each clearly written lesson. You will see how thoroughly the construction, operation and repair of electrical appliances are covered—not only small, portable appliances, but motors used in refrigeration and air conditioning, oil burners, power tools, etc. The principles of electricity are covered, also house wiring. This course prepares you to do hundreds of profitable jobs.

And—just as important—this booklet will tell you why and how you can profit by repairing electrical appliances. I have devoted several pages to the opportunities electrical appliance repair holds out to trained men. Please read them carefully.

[The second, third and fourth paragraphs sell the enclosed book. They give the reader powerful reasons why he should read it thoroughly.]

Have you ever taken a fan, iron, toaster, or other appliance for repair and envied the people who can charge so well for this work?

There's no need to envy his skill and "know how" as he makes a few tests, finds the trouble, and quickly makes the repair.

Learn this profitable trade yourself—put yourself in a position to demand good pay for your time—and do it quickly and easily by training at home in spare time.

What's more, begin soon to profit from your knowledge by repairing appliances for friends and neighbors. It is easy to build up a spare time business that can add materially to your income.

Before you finish the course you should earn more than the cost of your course. Further, the money you save by repairing your own appliances, and doing other electrical work in your home, can go a long way toward paying for your training.

Since there are so many millions of appliances, a spare time business can be expanded into a profitable full time business. There's nothing like the feeling of security and fearless independence that comes with knowing you have technical knowledge and skill that can earn a good living in a business of your own. You don't have to "please the boss" or fear layoffs or strikes.

As a rule, owners prefer to take their appliances to the point-of-purchase when they need repairs. But many appliance stores concentrate on selling; they do not maintain repair departments. I'll bet that's true right in your neighborhood. Here then is an opportunity to make excellent profits by doing repair work for such stores. The owners will be glad to know a well trained, reliable man to whom they can turn over these jobs. You can do them at home or in a shop without a "fancy front" where overhead is low. If you decide to sell new appliances yourself, your repair customers are good prospects.

[This fine letter rekindles the desire to take the course. NRI knows that the mailing of a coupon is not sufficient evidence of a burning desire to accept the schooling. The selling effort has just begun. After giving a strong sales talk on the course itself they use the following paragraphs to build the reader's pride . . . to show him the personal satisfaction this new career offers.]

Capable appliance servicemen are important. They are valued in every community because of the vital service they render. The success or failure of an appliance center or shop depends on their work. The modern home is "out-of-kilter" without his services . . . housekeeping and homemaking revolve around electric appliances being in good working order.

Automatic and self-regulating appliances such as washers, toasters, freezers, and others using thermostats, relays, timers, etc., are too complicated for tinkerers to service. Customers pay well for repairs, and expect expert work.

Therefore, shop owners want skilled, competent men whose work will please their customers and bring them back.

[Having sold the book, the advantages of a career as an electrical appliance serviceman, the monetary rewards, the personal satisfactions, the writer now asks for action.]

Begin training now. In a short time, gain technical knowledge and skill that can mean a good, secure future for you doing important, interesting work in a growing field.

The price of the course is low. Monthly tuition payments are low too, as you will see on the enclosed enrollment blank.

[The final three paragraphs were thoughtfully planned. The letter has three purposes: to sell the reading of the book; to build desire for the course and, at the same time, to make the readers see the wealth of warm, personal attention they'll be getting; to ask for action. See how effectively these objectives are handled.]

"How to Learn Servicing Electrical Appliances" tells you about my school and how, for more than forty years, I have been helping men achieve success through technical training.

I value the friendship of ambitious young men. It's my nature to be 100 percent for those who use their spare time for study to get ahead—to make something of themselves. I'll work hard to win and keep your friendship by giving you good service, by taking a personal interest in your problems, and by giving you thorough, carefully prepared training that gets results.

Send your enrollment today. There is a warm welcome waiting for you when you join the other ambitious NRI men preparing for a successful future Servicing Electrical Appliances.

Sincerely yours,

John F. Thompson
President

WHEN TO WRITE A LONG LETTER

Stop the next ten people you meet and ask, "Which do you think will do a better selling job, a short letter or a long one?"

The chances are that all ten of them will answer, without hesitation, "A short letter."

That is the most popular *mis*conception about business letters. A short letter is best when you can say your piece in a few words. A long letter is best when you have a long story to tell.

When members of the public accept advertised offers for information about John Nuveen & Company's tax-free investments, the company cannot assume that they have any degree of understanding about the subject. Investing is an intangible subject and one that makes most people excessively cautious and hungry for full information. This Nuveen letter reflects their understanding of those very human tendencies.

Dear Ms._____,

Your request for more information about your special reinvestment privilege is appreciated. In this period of brutal inflation and high taxes I share your desire to do everything possible to counter attack.

To clarify what is available to you here is a brief description of the essential difference between Nuveen Trusts (your present investment) and the Nuveen Municipal Bond Fund. Each time a Trust is organized we use our own capital to buy millions of dollars worth of assorted municipal issues. The completed investment is divided into $100 units and distributed to the public.

The Nuveen Municipal Bond Fund does not have a fixed number of shares. The public invests its money and the Fund managers use those dollars to invest in various municipal issues. For each new investment new shares are issued which makes it possible for Fund investors to reinvest their dividends.

Many Trust investors, not needing current income, welcome the idea of having their tax-free income ploughed back to earn additional income also free of federal income tax. But your Trust issued all of its shares at one time. There are none available for reinvestment. That is why we established a special vehicle which permits you to enjoy this highly desirable advantage.

Normally Fund investors pay a sales charge. There is a minimum initial investment of $1,000 and subsequent investments must be at least $100.

To solve the reinvestment problem for Trust investors we obtained special permission from the Securities & Exchange Commission to treat you in a special manner. If you instruct us to reinvest all of your Trust income in shares of the Fund it will be done for you automatically . . . until you tell us to start sending you checks again . . . and for you there is no sales charge. For you the minimums do not apply.

Here is an example of how your exercise of this special privilege can increase your tax-free yield . . .

As you know, one of the attractions of your Trust income is that it is relatively stable. You know what you have. Fund income, however, varies. For this example we will assume a Trust income of 6½ percent. While there is no way of knowing what Fund income may be over any future span of time, we have assumed an average annual yield of no more than 5 percent. (It could be more or less, there are no guarantees.) At the end of ten years, thanks to compounding, the investor would be receiving $838 for each $10,000 in the account . . . a yield of 8.38 percent free of federal income tax.

You can take advantage of this exclusive privilege by completing the enclosed form and mailing it in the addressed, postage-paid envelope.

Sincerely,

When you are selling an intangible, you have to do a lot of telling. A correspondence course is an intangible too. It is not like a hammer, which you can show and describe in a few succinct sentences. If prospects are thinking about spending a fair sum of money and devoting a lot of spare time to a correspondence course, they must be given reasons to believe that they have a very complete picture of what their investment of time and money will bring them.

NRI's two-page letter is mailed out with a 32-page catalog and a 40-page sample lesson. Why do they write so much? Simply because, over the years, they've learned that a complete portrayal of their offering will bring them more students than a brief portrayal.

Read their letter a second time. Analyse the thinking behind its construction. They start out reminding Paul Prospect that he requested the booklet. They emphasize the fact that they hurried to respond to his important request . . . "Your inquiry arrived today."

Your letter emphasizes the benefits. Then the letter goes on to point out the highlights and the values of the material he is about to read. The letter reminds him that the facts he'll gain from reading the booklet can mean *profits* for him. He is given a word picture of being in his own business, of being able to build up a part-time occupation if he isn't interested in a fulltime career. It explores for him the breadth of opportunity lying before him. It builds his ego, tells him how important he'll be in his community.

Your letter asks for action. And then the letter hammers away at the importance of making an affirmative decision now. An added measure of confidence is built into the closing paragraphs by telling readers of the character and tradition of the school and the personal interest that will be taken in them, as individuals.

Yes, it's a long letter, but can you point to any of the elements listed above that could be removed *without taking away from the effective force of that letter*? Each is important. Each does its job of selling.

Explore your literature for the SELL points. Those are the elements that should appear in your covering letter. You can't afford to leave your fate in the hands of the reader. Your reader may or may not translate a volume of words to the key issues. And you shouldn't expect anyone to do so. That's your job.

Your literature may contain every key factor that can help to sell your product or service, but casual readers may miss the very one that would inspire them to go ahead with the proposition. That's why, in your covering letter, you must take each of those key appeals and isolate them.

A letter that invites the reading of a multipage booklet. Let's take a look at still another NRI letter. This is the one they use when they get coupons asking for the free booklet on their Television-Audio Servicing course.

Dear Friend:

Thank you for your inquiry which arrived today. Here is your copy of my catalog, "How to be a Success in Television−Audio." Your sample lesson is also enclosed.

The NRI courses, Television−Audio SERVICING and Complete COMMUNICATIONS, are described and outlined.

Your first and most important question may be: "What can I gain by learning Television−Audio Servicing?"

You stand to gain a great deal, probably much more than you expect, by learning Television−Audio SERVICING or Complete COMMUNICATIONS.

For example, the NRI course in Television−Audio SERVICING shows you how to start making $20 or $25 a week extra money fixing receivers in spare time, beginning soon after enrolling. Notice you are ready to make extra money in spare time while training for well-paying, full time jobs, for a business of your own, a Television−Audio service shop or store.

Or, if you prefer, you can train to get into Broadcasting, Ship, Police, Aviation, or some other fascinating branch of Communications as an operator or technician.

Whether you choose SERVICING or COMMUNICATIONS, you stand to win pleasant, fascinating work in an industry with a future.

You stand to win a job that can lead to freedom from money worries and win for you the respect and consideration that comes to a successful man. In fact, you stand to gain the things that making good money means—comforts, luxuries, security.

You needn't take my word for this. Read the many letters from NRI graduates printed in my school catalog. Let them be your guide.

Even if you have been following the progress of Television−Audio only casually, you know that by preparing now, you can get into a rapidly growing industry. You know that BIG THINGS are ahead for Television−Audio.

More than 28,000,000 TV receivers are in use now. More than three hundred Television Stations are on the air—and since the Federal

Communications Commission lifted the "freeze" on new stations hundreds of applications to build new TV Stations have been filed with the FCC. We can expect two thousand new TV Stations to be put on the air within the next few years. This is a vital, new booming phase of the Audio industry, bringing millions of dollars—and thousands of good jobs.

In coming years, there is every reason to expect the entire Television—Audio industry to keep going ahead—to keep growing. More trained men will be needed at good pay. More opportunities will open. Greater amounts of money spent in the industry will bring greater prosperity for men working in it.

Now you may be wondering, "What does all this talk about Television, FM, and fixing radios mean to me in job opportunities, good pay, security?" My catalog will show you!

Also, this catalog will tell you about our courses, lesson examinations service, consultation service, experiment kits, etc.

Please read every page of my catalog carefully. When you have done so you will agree, I believe, that the price is low for what you can gain. NRI training will cost you much, much less than many Television—Audio Technicians earn in a single month. Monthly terms are low too.

It has been a genuine pleasure to write you like this. I want to help you to make good because every successful graduate is a good advertisement for NRI. I want you to secceed and be a credit to this school.

One thing I value particularly. It is the friendship of a person with ambition. Friendship has to be earned, so when you become my student I will cheerfully accept the job of winning your friendship, by keeping you well supplied with lessons, by giving you good service, and in other ways win your good will.

Simply fill in the enclosed enrollment blank for the course you want—SERVICING or COMMUNICATIONS. Choose the plan of payment that suits you—and send it in. The Action Learning Kit is ready to be sent to you.

Getting started with your NRI course should mean much to you . . . a promising future; and the satisfaction, honor, and pay that come to a man qualified to render a much needed service.

So enroll promptly. Let's work together and set as our goal a thorough knowledge of Radio-Television—winning good pay and a bright future for you.

Yours for good pay, advancement, and security in Radio and Television.

J.E. Smith
President

WHEN A COUPON INVITES A SALESPERSON TO CALL

There are many things that are sold best when a flesh and blood salesperson arrives on the scene. Perhaps some people will buy by mail, but more people will buy when the salesperson is on the spot, able to answer their questions, demonstrate, and overcome any objections.

But before you or I will open our doors to these salespeople, we must have a strong desire for the product or service being offered.

PAVE THE WAY FOR THE SALESPERSON'S CALL

To put a lubricant on the hinges to your door and mine, many companies find that it pays to advertise the offer of a free catalog, descriptive booklet, or even a sample.

In some cases the coupon requests are handled by having the local representative deliver the requested literature in person. Some advertisers feel that people are not prepared to accept a salesperson at their homes or places of business. These advertisers make a point of saying that the literature will be mailed.

If you'll mail the literature, say so. The letter that rides with the literature, in this case, has an added mission. The letter must sell the literature and must also sell the salesperson who will appear on the scene later. This is often called a "Precall" letter. A major company handles it this way.

Many thanks for requesting,
"Look at Tomorrow Today" . . .

> We believe you will find thought-provoking the enclosed booklet, "Look at Tomorrow Today" . . .
>
> As you read your copy of the booklet, you may recognize some situations that mirror your own thoughts and your own circumstances. We hope so, for if you do, it will be that much more valuable to you.
>
> Our company has grown to its present great size and strength because it believes that your needs for insured protection are highly individual. What is ideal for your neighbor may fall short of the goal for you. Our representatives are schooled in exploring with you the ambitions and the dreams you cherish and the resources you have which, combined with the company's flexible programs, can come closest to bringing these ambitions and dreams to reality.

Right in your own community there are trained men and women who have the skill, the understanding, and the interest to help you. They'll welcome the opportunity to give you the same kind of service we provided in the actual case histories set forth in "Look at Tomorrow Today."

With this letter you'll find an addressed and postage-free card. Just put on that card the most convenient time and place for your local representative to call.

Sincerely,

Precall letters are brief. The letter and the literature have a single mission, when your target is getting your salesperson together with the prospect. You want to sell *desire*.

That's quite different than selling the product or service. In this case you can lose by telling too much. You cannot afford to give prospects the feeling that they know the whole story. If they get that impression they have no motivation to agree to meet the salesperson. Right or wrong, they feel that the salesperson has nothing to tell that they do not already know.

Precall letters cloak the salesperson with benefits. If they are to accomplish their real purpose, your precall letters must give readers the feeling that they have much to gain, and nothing to lose, if they agree to a sales call. The salesperson is presented as someone who will come to them with interesting and helpful information. The salesperson is shown to be an educator—a giver of personal service. If this portrait can be conveyed successfully, as was done in the precall letter you just read, the fear of a high pressure, fast talker is eliminated.

Letters of the type shown above have a fundamental objective: induce the reader to take the action that will open the door for a salesperson's call.

Wilson, MacKay & Co., an investment dealer and stock brokerage firm, handles a different objective with this letter and phone call:

Your copy of A FEW REASONS WHY . . .

. . . was hurried to you the moment your welcome request reached us. Thank you for permitting us to send it to you.

"A Few Reasons Why So Many People Have Bought Mutual Funds" tells a dramatic and fascinating story of a form of investment that has been accepted by millions of your fellow Americans. It tells how these folks are receiving part ownership in scores of big corporations. You'll see how you too can put your dollars to work in American industry.

In a few days I'm going to phone you with the hope that I may be able to answer any of your questions. I look forward to the pleasure of talking with you.

Sincerely,

In Chapter 9, "Put an Action Close in Your Letters," you saw how effectively you can use the concept of announcing that you will phone to make an appointment. The suggested words to use when you make the call were included in the example. The closing statement in the letter above has a different slant. It is not intended to set up a meeting. That makes the phone dialogue somewhat different.

Ms. _____, this is (your name and your company's name). I appreciated your asking for our booklet on mutual fund investing. By now you have the booklet and my letter. Ms. _____, if you'll tell me the type of mutual fund that comes closest to your needs and desires I will select a fund of that type that we have researched and know thoroughly. You'll receive a free prospectus and our suggestions as to how you may adopt that fund as an important part of your personal financial plan.

What type of fund interests you most: income, growth, or capital preservation?''

Although you can handle some of their questions on the phone, there are many aspects of the business being discussed that can be dealt with far better, from their viewpont, if you and the prospects meet and have a full discussion. At such meetings they can see additional literature, samples, testimonials, or what-have-you.

MAIN CONSIDERATIONS IN HANDLING COUPON REQUESTS FOR LITERATURE

1. Fill the request immediately—the same day it reaches you, if possible.
2. Always send a covering letter with the requested matter.
3. With typewriter type and a colored signature, make the letter look

personal even though it is a form letter that doesn't carry the prospect's name.

4. The covering letter should sell the requested literature.

5. The letter should ask for and spell out the action you want taken.

6. The letter should set the stage, building the reader up to eager anticipation.

7. The letter should be long if you have a lot to say.

8. The letter should point out the highlights embodied in the literature.

9. The letter should translate the message in the literature to the benefits of taking action now.

10. The precall letter paves the way for a salesperson's call.

11. The precall letter should sell the salesperson as well as the literature.

12. The precall letter should be brief.

13. The precall letter can be used to pave the way for a follow-up phone call requesting an appointment.

11

HOW PRODUCT
INFORMATION INQUIRIES
ARE HANDLED

A variety of viewpoints must be examined when considering the broad question of handling inquiries about products and services. There is no pat, single answer. What you are selling; how distribution is handled; whether you sell direct or through local retailers; the complexity of your offer; the amount of business and profit at stake—each of these calls for a different method of handling.

A few things are uniform.

Speed of reply is always vital. In the chapter on, "How to Handle Responses to Advertising," you saw *why* speed is so immensely important. The same considerations apply when you receive a direct inquiry about your product or service, but more so. Responses to advertising may stem from any of a variety of stimuli: impulse, idle curiosity, a competitor wanting to know what you are up to, a lonely soul who likes to get mail, and so on. But when an inquiry comes to you out of the blue, unrelated to any specific advertising effort, there is a strong possibility that it was inspired by a current need, possibly a pressing need. People who take the trouble to write such letters of inquiry have more than idle curiosity. They want information and they want it *now*.

Don't keep them waiting. They want the information *now*, not in two or three weeks.

Let the speed of your reply demonstrate *your* appreciation and your interest in *them*.

Remind people that they asked. In a few cases, this is not essential. In most cases it is. If you are in the travel business and you get a letter that says, "My wife and I have been dreaming about a cruise around the world," there is no need to remind this man that he wrote to you. He and his wife talk about that letter at breakfast and dinner each day till your answer arrives. It is a big moment in their lives. But if an inquiry about office machines is written by the purchasing agent of a big corporation, your reply must begin with a reminder of the request, or your letter may be regarded as an unsolicited sales pitch. It may not get the attention it merits.

An exceptionally big and successful user of mail order sent me a number of examples of the letters they send to their "coupon clippers." He said, "You will notice that we are 'Here's the material' slap-happy. It is an informal technique that seems to work." This pro, and everyone else in the profession of creating direct mail and business letters, believes in testing. When he says, ". . . seems to work," he means that carefully controlled tests proved that letters starting in this manner produced *better* results than those that didn't.

To personalize or not to personalize. Few questions about mass letter writing are more popular. To personalize a letter means to include the name and address of the recipient. Sometimes this is done by actually typing each letter. Where a greater volume of identical letters are going out it may be handled by the use of letter writing equipment. Many firms, however, find that they can get fine results without investing the time and money required by *any* type of personalization. They use a *benefit caption* where the personalization normally would appear. You'll see many examples of *benefit captions* in this and other chapters.

Once more we'll quote our friend, the successful mail order pro, "There was a time when we used to personalize most reply letters. In recent years we have developed the theory that the main thing the inquirer is interested in is to get what he has asked for quickly and courteously. We have therefore shifted to date fill-ins—*anything that will enable us to date it and get it in the mail the same day the inquiry comes in.*" A "date fill-in" is another term for a *benefit caption.*

As anyone with an address knows, highly personalized mass mailings have come into their own. Computer letters and electronic letters have enabled bulk mailers to insert your name, your address, and facts about you in various parts of their mailings, including the mailing envelope and the reply form.

Computer letters can provide fill-ins on preprinted mailing pieces, or can type the personalized materials in full. Up to 10,000 letters can be filled-in per hour on fan-fold paper. The newer innovation—electronic letters—takes either of two forms. One is called "ink jet" and the other, "electrophotographic." Ink jet employs wet ink sprayed under electronic control to form the images on the paper. Electrophotographic transfers dry ink to paper by an electronic process combining heat and pressure. The speed of ink jet is amazing. Over 52,000 fully typed 8½ x 11 letters can be produced per hour. Electrophotographic letters are fully typed at 10,000 per hour. At such speeds large quantities of personalized mail can be produced very economically.

TYING IN LOCAL DISTRIBUTOR AND DEALER

Armstrong Cork Company ties in local dealers with this letter.

Dear _____,

Thank you for your request for more information about our ceilings. The enclosed brochures will help acquaint you with our wide selection of problem solving ceilings and installation systems. We hope you'll take the next step by visiting your nearest Armstrong Ceilings retailer for more information about our ceilings and how to put them up.

Some dealers near you are: [A list of local dealers and their addresses.]

For locations of other retailers in your area who sell Armstrong Ceilings, check the Yellow Pages of your telephone directory under "Ceilings." Your retailer will be happy to show you actual samples and answer questions you may have. He can provide you with more detailed installation information, including a demonstration.

Very truly yours,

Harold R. Keller
Consumer Services

Armstrong not only leads those who inquire to the local resources for their products, the company gives sound reasons why it will benefit the potential customer to deal with the local people.

Many companies do not sell their products directly to consumers. When they receive an inquiry they must handle it in a way that maintains the prospect's interest, steers them to a retail store, but doesn't lose the goodwill of one store the customer may deal with, by innocently naming a competitor. Here's how one manufacturer deals with these complications.

Dear Miss Pink:

Thank you very much for your letter of August 2 and for your interest in our products.

The Company does indeed manufacture an electric dehumidifier of the type you describe and one should be available from a retailer near you. To insure the best possible handling of your request, I am forwarding a copy of your letter to the Company's Appliance Division manager in your area. He will be able to tell you whether the dehumidifier is suitable for the particular application you have in mind, and to provide you with the name of the dealer most convenient to your home.

We trust that this newest of the Company's products will prove a happy solution to the problem you describe in your letter.

Sincerely yours,

Nothing is left to chance. The reply is immediate. The extra service and the fine tone of the letter are calculated to delight Miss Pink. The company official will be able to learn where she usually deals and thus avoid the possibility of inadvertently leading her away from one good Westinghouse dealer to a competitor. The letter is a very neat package with every bow tied.

COMPLETING THE SALE BY MAIL

All of the letters you have read in this chapter have contemplated a meeting between the inquirer and a local representative. They have been fairly brief letters. Letters of that type do not call for a great deal of effort to give the reader details of the product or service. That's the job of the local representative. When the sale is to be consummated by mail, however, it becomes necessary to tell a great deal more. The opportunity for the give-and-take of a face-to-face meeting is not present. Writers must anticipate every logical question and objection that might arise were they to meet the person they are talking with by mail. They must present every possible benefit in their letter and must make a strong appeal for immediate action.

Boyce Morgan was one of the most highly regarded creative professionals in the field of selling by mail. At one point he played a major role in the outstanding success of Kiplinger's Letters. Later in his career, he developed a newsletter service called *Better Business by Telephone*. Boyce Morgan and his excellent newsletter are gone, but the skills and experience evidenced in the way he handled inquiries endure. Here is an example of how to make a long letter interesting enough to hold a reader's full attention.

Thank you, Mr. Jones . . .

. . . for your inquiry about Better Business by Telephone. I'm very glad to send you samples, and to explain the job we do for our clients.

As I know you realize, the telephone is regarded all too often as just another piece of office equipment. And because it is taken for granted, employees receive little training in its use. Without realizing it, they often use it in ways that irritate customers, create ill will, actually lose sales, and drive business away.

For the past six years, Better Business by Telephone has been published for just one purpose—to help correct this situation, and enable you to get maximum return from your investment in telephone service.

Better Business by Telephone is built around our twice-monthly Bulletins, which you receive on the 10th and 25th of each month. These Bulletins give you a constant flow of ideas for using your business telephones more effectively and more economically.

You get case histories that spell out methods successfully followed by other companies. You get every sort of business telephone problem outlined, analyzed, and solved. You get cost-cutting ideas, business-building ideas, ideas for smoothing out the rough spots in your routine telephone procedures, suggestions on equipment, suggestions for building good will and better public relations on every phone call you handle.

Practically all our Bulletins include a "FoneTalk"—a short piece aimed either at helping your employees deal with one common telephone situation, or cultivating in them a better overall attitude toward telephone usage. Many companies order extra copies of these FoneTalks for distribution throughout their offices, or arrange to reproduce them regularly in their house organs.

You also receive periodic Special Reports and Supplements, covering certain phases of telephone usage at greater length than the Bulletin permits, or giving you memos, forms, etc., used by other companies. All past Special Reports and Supplements—as well as past issues of the regular Bulletin—are available to you as a subscriber at little or no cost.

But for many subscribers, the most valuable part of Better Business by Telephone is our free mail consultation service. At any time you can write us about any telephone problem you may have, and get a special, individual solution. Typical of the reaction of subscribers to this part of our service is this recent comment from the head of a life insurance agency . . .

That was the finest, most helpful letter I have received in a long, long time. Your suggested phone procedure has been tried out and it has been working beautifully. Thanks not only from me, but from all my associates here. I think you have given us not only a good telephone technique, but a sales idea that is so obvious we have overlooked it.

More than 14,000 companies have already used our service. Included are many of the big names of American business—DuPont, Ford, Texas Company, General Electric, American Airlines, Sears Roebuck, the Baltimore & Ohio Railroad, Westinghouse, etc. But we've helped many more small companies in every line you can think of—wholesale, retail, manufacturing, transportation, service businesses, institutions, professional men, government, etc.

As for our charges, they are low for a service of this kind. A basic single-copy subscription to Better Business by Telephone is $3 a month and that includes the regular Bulletin and "FoneTalk," all Special Reports and Supplements as issued, and our free consultation service. Extra Bulletins for other executives and employees are reasonable. (See enclosed Order Form.)

And you can order Better Business by Telephone on either an annual or a till-forbid basis, whichever you prefer. As an annual subscriber, you get a 6 percent discount and a free binder for your Bulletins. On the till-forbid basis, we simply bill you quarterly as you use the service. In either case you can stop service at any time merely by giving us 30 days notice. We want you to be the judge of its continuing usefulness to you.

Recently we have been making a special offer to new subscribers—a Bonus Portfolio of some of our past Special Reports and Bulletins which have proved particularly valuable to subscribers. We still have a limited number of these Portfolios on hand, and we'll be glad to include one as part of your subscription. It's a worthwhile bonus, because it includes material that originally cost subscribers a minimum of $9.00.

It would be a real pleasure to add you to our list of clients, and I think our service would quickly pay its way for you. Just specify the number of copies of each Bulletin you will need, and return the order form in the enclosed business reply envelope. We'll send you the Bonus Portfolio with our compliments and start regular service immediately.

Sincerely yours,

Boyce Morgan
President

Only a two word fill-in personalizes this letter, but the tone of the letter is immensely personal. This is achieved by the excellent use of the words "you and I." It is a letter from one human being to another. But there is very little of the "I." Notice how Boyce Morgan avoided saying, "We do this, we do that, we send you." Instead you'll find countless "You get, you receive, you may have, your employees."

Boyce Morgan's letter is a brilliant example of the practical application of the *"4-P formula:"* Picture, Promise, Prove, and Push. That is just one of the reasons why it will pay you to go back and read his letter several times.

Notice how the use of the 4-P formula develops a very sound sequence of ideas.

Mr. Jones, after being reminded that this is information he requested, has his anxiety prodded: the realization that he has a problem that must be solved, by the *picture* Boyce Morgan created. Jones can visualize the employees who handle phone calls badly. He can see how their untutored tactics are turning customers and prospective customers away, costing his company significant sums. He sees that all of this is due to the lack of proper training in telephone technique.

Following is the *promise* that the service offered can stop those losses; can turn the handling of phone calls into a source of good will and profits. And then, starting with the indented paragraph, Mr. Jones is given *proof* . . . reasons why he can believe the promise that his problem can be solved.

Finally, with the details of the offer, comes the all-important *push*.

Observe how smoothly the letter flows from paragraph to paragraph, through the use of well thought out connecting language.

The last paragraph performs the role it should with excellent style. It tells you precisely what to do if you want to capture the many benefits that have been outlined in the letter. The concluding sentence reminds you of the fine bonus that has been promised and suggests action now via the final word, "immediately."

The Kiplinger Washington Editors, publishers of Changing Times Magazine, respond to subscription inquiries with this appeal.

Dear Miss Smith:

Thank you for your interest in our CHANGING TIMES Magazine. A complimentary copy is being mailed under separate cover.

CHANGING TIMES is a monthly publication and our subscription rates are $12 for one year, $21 for two years or $29 for three years.

Your subscription will include a free copy of the new edition of Kiplinger's Family Success Book, "99 New Ideas on Your Money, Job, and Living."

You'll use this information-packed book as a guide in handling your personal finances, buying more intelligently, investing more profitably and enjoying a better future.

The Family Success Book is Kiplinger's way of giving you a practical send-off down the road to better living. Each new issue of CHANGING TIMES will suggest new ways to earn more, save more, and live better.

We will be pleased to send the magazine to you. An order form and reply envelope are enclosed for your convenience in ordering.

Sincerely yours,

Lee Hall
Subscriber Service

The personalized letter uses a full arsenal of reasons why Miss Smith should subscribe. She is given a complimentary copy of the publication, shown how she can take advantage of dollar-saving rates, offered a free book with an alluring title, reminded that the issues of Changing Times will enable her to "earn more, save more, live better." The final paragraph asks for action by pointing out the convenient order form and reply envelope riding with the letter.

POINTS TO KEEP IN MIND WHEN REPLYING TO LETTERS INQUIRING ABOUT YOUR PRODUCTS OR SERVICES

1. Answer in a hurry.
2. Remind writers that they inquired.
3. If you don't personalize your letter, use a "benefit caption."
4. Protect your local distributor.
5. Where needed, sell the importance to the reader of a home or office demonstration.
6. Use the letter to sell the local representative.
7. To complete the sale by mail don't hesitate to write a long letter, if a long letter is needed to cover all your selling points.
8. Handle technical explanations in a nontechnical manner. Keep it simple, understandable, and exciting.
9. Don't attempt to answer all classes of inquiries with a uniform letter. Analyze your inquiries and break them down to categories with logical, satisfying replies for each category.
10. If anything about your product or service can lend itself to

showmanship on paper, make use of that showmanship in your letter.

11. Don't be content with one convincing sales point if you have others in reserve.

12. If you can enclose a sample that can be seen or tested, by all means take advantage of the opportunity.

12

REPLYING
TO CUSTOMER COMMENTS
AND SERVICE REQUESTS

American Airlines provides every passenger with a blank letter form that invites them to write their views on the Company's services and facilities. Even though they lack the ease and stimulus of an easy-to-use form, there are many others who obey the impulse to sit down to praise or to sound off. As a result, the Dallas—Fort Worth headquarters of the airline receives vast quantities of letters every day. The volume is so great that a staff of eight people is kept busy replying to those letters.

Eugene M. Dieringer headed that department while information was being gathered for this book. On his desk, each morning, he finds a foot-high stack of letters from passengers. The attitude he takes toward his work permeates his entire department. When he talks to his writers he conveys his own viewpoint and enthusiasm.

Mr. Dieringer picks up a letter at random. "I haven't read this letter yet," he says, "but I see it is from a Mrs. Green in Chicago. Maybe she has written to praise us for the fine service or fine food she had on her recent flight. Maybe she is raising a fuss with us because weather conditions made it necessary for us to delay or cancel her flight. It doesn't matter. I love Mrs. Green.

"I have a nice home. There's a late model car in the garage. My wife, children, and I have good food on our table. We dress well and enjoy life. And all of that is because Mrs. Green and thousands like her take the time and trouble to write to American Airlines."

With that attitude, Mr. Dieringer and his staff reply to the endless flow of letters that come to them. The writer may heap totally unwarranted abuse on their heads, but these correspondents are never tempted to write a sharp reply. They love the people to whom they write. They are grateful to these people. They do their utmost to see things from the other fellow's point of view. They try to understand why someone is upset or concerned. They take the trouble to dig for full information. Their letters are sympathetic, friendly, and satisfying.

Here are some typical letters written by these professional writers of replies:

Dear Mr. D_____,

Thank you for your note to me during your flight with us from Phoenix to Dallas – Fort Worth. I am sorry you have been inconvenienced because the final call for flights is made a few minutes before the plane is actually ready to depart.

There are several reasons for this. One is to make sure that all passengers for a flight get on board—as you know, many people will delay until the last minute for a final word with family or friends. While this is understandable, it does complicate on-time departures. Another reason is that until all confirmed passengers are on board, we cannot accommodate standbys in case there are extra seats.

It is a pleasure to serve you and we look forward to many more opportunities to do so.

Sincerely yours,

Eugene M. Dieringer
Director
Consumer Relations

Good technique in handling an adverse comment. It pays to repeat the criticism and then to offer a full and logical explanation.

Dear Mrs. R_____,

Your flight attendant told me of the interruption in your flight from Los Angeles to Dallas-Fort Worth because the air conditioning system was not working properly. I am sorry that this happened and hope the delay did not inconvenience you too much.

The flight attendants were especially grateful that you and other passengers were so pleasant about this incident, despite the fact that the return to Los Angeles and change in equipment made your dinner so late.

It is a pleasure to serve you and I hope that your future flights with us will operate as planned.

Sincerely yours,

Eugene M. Dieringer
Director
Consumer Relations

Mrs. R_____ is shown that the writer took the time and trouble to get the full story. That makes her feel important and well pleased with the company that regards her complaint worthy of full investigation.

Fine letters like these make lasting friends. Here are a few samples of the replies American Airlines inspire:

Dear Mr. Dieringer:

Your courteous letter of September 21, regarding the inconvenience experienced on my recent flight from New York is very much appreciated.

The cause of the trouble was weather and the flight attendant, whose name I do not recall, handled everyone on the ship in a masterful fashion in all ways. Everyone on the ship was most impressed, and I should have written you sooner to commend her excellent service.

Very truly yours,

Dear Mr. Smith:

Thank you for your letter of September 21.

I wish to express my appreciation and that of the other members of our organization for the fine and courteous service we have received from American Airlines.

We know that American will always remain tops in air transportation.

Very truly yours,

When a Customer Asks a Tough Question. Traditionally, magazines attempt to build circulation by making attractive "introductory offers:" reduced price, trial subscriptions, and more. Inevitably some long-term, regular subscribers receive mailings intended for non-subscribers. Some become upset by the fact that they have just renewed for a higher price than a newcomer is asked to pay. The magazine gets a letter asking why?

Here is how Kiplinger answers such letters:

Dear Mr. Smith:

Thanks very much for your letter about the rates for CHANGING TIMES.

There is not only logic but sentiment on the side of your suggestion that we reduce rates to our old subscribers, instead of to our new ones. But the sad hard economic facts of the operation dictate otherwise.

We use a reduced-rate trial subscription because constant experimentation has shown us that this is the best and cheapest way to get new subscribers who will eventually stay with us on a full-term basis for several years.

We lose money—in fact, considerable money—on every trial rate subscription we sell. However, at the end of the introductory period, enough of these "trial" subscribers continue as regular subscribers so that we eventually get back the loss.

Practically all of our CHANGING TIMES subscribers are obtained through our special reduced rate trial subscription. In fact, you originally subscribed in this way and took advantage of the special offer.

Personally, I'd prefer it if we could sell all new subscriptions at full rates. But extensive testing of all kinds of offers has shown us that the most economical way we have to add new subscriptions is by offering the reduced rate trial, and then "converting" as high a percentage of the trial subscribers as possible to full-term subscribers.

That is the reason—and the only reason—that we follow this procedure.

Thanks again for writing. I'm glad to have had this opportunity to explain the situation to you.

> Sincerely,
>
> Lee Hall
> Subscriber Service

Have you noticed how this excellent letter uses the exact technique you read about in the chapter, "If You Must Say "No," Smile"?

It starts and ends thanking the customer for complaining, and agreeing that it is a justified complaint. It is a relatively long letter, going into much detail as to why it makes good economic sense to solicit new subscriptions the way they do. The writer takes the subscriber into his confidence. He lets Mr. Smith know that they actually lose money on each new, special price subscription, but that experience has proven that, in the long run, renewals make the initial loss worth taking.

The key paragraph, that should take any wind left in any sub-scriber's sails, is the fourth from the end. Mr. Smith is reminded that he started his subscription by taking advantage of a reduced rate offer.

And Kiplinger responds to another type of subscriber complaint with this gem:

Dear Mr. Smith:

We are glad to have this opportunity to answer your letter regarding delivery of your CHANGING TIMES magazine.

The post office did return several mailings to us as undeliverable. For this reason, service was discontinued.

Your subscription has been reentered at the address to which we are writing. Service has been extended through August 1980 to compensate for missed issues.

If delivery problems persist, we will ask our Traffic Manager to check on them.

Your interest in our publication is appreciated, and we are anxious that future service be satisfactory.

Sincerely yours,

Lee Hall
Subscriber Service

Read between the lines of this one and you will see why I called it a "gem." Brother Smith, clearly, never bothered to let the magazine know that he had changed his address. The new address was revealed to them, for the first time, when he wrote to complain about nondelivery.

The reply he got not only avoided blaming or embarrassing him, it shouldered the time and expense of the research involved and, on top of that, told him that they were going to compensate him for the missed issues by extending his subscription.

Just as their answer to the reduced rate letter drew open the technique for a "No" letter, this reply used the technique for writing a "Yes" letter. Do more than give the customer what is requested—give something extra.

GOING TO EXTREMES TO GIVE SERVICE

Some customers, on the basis that they *are* customers, feel that they can look to their resources for time-consuming counsel and guidance on a variety of subjects. In many cases the questions they raise are not even related to the products or services they purchase from the resource.

Not all companies are equipped to, or willing to, accept such burdens. Others recognize burdensome requests of that type as genuine "calls for help" and a desirable opportunity to build customers loyalty.

NCR Corporation, Clayton, Ohio, believes in giving its customers guidance on sound business practices. It does so to an unusual extent and does it very well. In NCR's magazine-style publication called "Credits and Collections," a broad variety of related subjects are discussed in clear, nontechnical language. Included are a selection of suggested letter merchants are free to use to collect past due accounts, and for other purposes. The letters are extremely well written. Here, along with their comments, are some of the letters they offer:

> Following is a series of four letters designed to pull in payments. In each letter the amount owing is mentioned. With the fourth letter a statement of the account should be enclosed. For best results, this last letter should be sent by registered mail with a return receipt demand.

First Letter

Dear Mr. Bryan,

The fact that your account of $_____ is considerably past due was brought to my attention today.

We know, of course, that your credit is good. But you can appreciate that we cannot keep our prices right and at the same time have our money tied up beyond a reasonable length of time.

That is why it is necessary that a time limit be set and maintained for all outstanding accounts.

Your check by return mail will help us in our efforts to serve you and our other patrons as efficiently as possible.

Thank you,

Second Letter

Dear Mr. Bryan,

We were surprised and disappointed at not hearing from you after we had called your attention to the fact that your account of $_____ is long overdue.

As we explained in our letter, the best interests of ALL our customers oblige us to limit the time that these accounts run.

Perhaps you were away and did not get the letter; we feel sure that you would want to cooperate with us (by living up to the letter of your agreement).

In any case, just drop your check in the mail now. Better still, come into the store, clear up this little matter, (and take a look at our new Spring suitings).

Sincerely yours,

[*Note:* Use the part of paragraph three in parenthesis only in case some kind of written agreement has been signed. In paragraph four, change the line to fit the business or occasion.]

Third Letter

Dear Sir:

We have written you twice without result regarding your account of $_____, which is now long past due.

In view of the time already granted, and of our previously friendly reminders, you will not think us too insistent when we now request an immediate settlement.

However, if sickness or any other misfortune is responsible for your failure to settle this account, you will not find us unreasonable if you just let us know how you stand.

All we ask is that you treat us as you would wish us to treat you. That's only fair, isn't it?

We shall expect to hear from you at once!

Earnestly yours,

Fourth Letter

Dear Sir:

You have paid no attention to our letters, even though we made it clear that we were more than willing to do our part in making it easy for you to settle your past-due account of $_____.

Inasmuch as you show no willingness to meet us halfway, you compel us to adopt the only other course possible.

This letter is our final effort to save you embarrassment and loss. You have until (name date—one week later) to settle your account or to personally give us sufficient reason why we should give you more time.

If you do not do this by (date), your account will be handed over to our attorneys for due legal process.

Very truly yours,

Statement enclosed.

"Here," says NCR, "are three more letters, each of which is a friendly reminder. They are written in a understanding vein to avoid any suggestion of dunning. These are offered to be used singly—never as a series."

Dear Mr. Jones,

In business there are some things we just have to do. One is ask for money.

We don't like to remind anyone of payment due on an account, but the plain fact of the matter is that all of us forget on occasion.

In our usual bookkeeping routine we noticed that your account of $_____ was due last Monday. Thus, this reminder.

If you've already placed your check in the mail, please ignore this letter. And, if you haven't as yet—well, we're enclosing an envelope for that purpose. No stamp needed, you'll notice.

Thanks again for your continued patrongage.

Cordially yours,

Dear Mrs. Allen,

Don't you hate to hear the ring of the alarm clock early in the morning? I do. I suspect my reason is that I dislike to be reminded of an obligation.

I guess that's common with everybody. We all have a feeling of irritation when reminded of something we might overlook or forget.

So, I want you to know that I don't like to remind you of the account of $_____ that was due a few days ago. But, like the alarm clock, I must speak my piece.

If you've already placed your check in the mail, please ignore this note and consider it bookkeeping on our part.

And, thank you!

Sincerely yours,

P.S. I'm sure we'll both continue to dislike—but recognize the necessity of—pesky reminder devices. Right?

Dear Mr. Hubbard,

Each day we check our accounts. Good business demands that we know how we stand at all times.

Good business also requires that we remind those whose payments for monthly purchases have not yet reached us.

So we are merely following policy in mentioning your account to you. We always hesitate doing this to our good customers, but, as we say, it's a necessary part of our usual procedure.

Maybe you've already put your check in the mail. If so, just forget you've received this letter.

Cordially yours,

"The honest but financially embarrassed customer," NCR adds, "will in most cases explain his situation and ask for a longer period. It is fairly safe to assume that debtors who do not make any response to letters deserve no further consideration."

Study those NCR-created letters thoughtfully. Notice how they go to great lengths to save the delinquent customers embarrassment. They even offer reasons why they have not met their obligations. At the same time the needed pressure is present. Intelligently prepared collection letters, such as these, can accomplish the two-fold objective of collecting while retaining good will. And that is a good trick.

REPLIES TO CUSTOMER COMMENTS AND SERVICE REQUESTS SHOW THE IMPORTANCE OF THESE ELEMENTS

1. Regardless of the tone or content of the letter you receive, be sincerely grateful to the writer.

2. When a customer asks for help, give your utmost in the reply regardless of how busy you may be.

3. Answer difficult customer complaints or questions as you would respond to a "No" letter, as detailed in Chapter 5.

4. When customer complaints prove to be attributable to their own errors, do not accuse or embarrass.

13

EXTRA MILEAGE
FROM A "GIVE-AWAY"
OFFER

The manufacturers of a nationally distributed household product assigned me to write a letter for them. They had gone to great expense to have their advertising agency prepare a fine book about entertaining in the home. The book was created so that it could be offered as a give-away in the company's national magazine ads. The company asked the public to send fifty cents to cover pastage.

The fifty-cent charge is a sound idea in many cases. The book and the handling of the inquiry represent considerable expense. If the books were offered free, many of the requests would come from children and others who were not likely prospects for the company's products. The small fee does a more important job than helping to defray the investment. It qualifies the prospects, thus making a little more certain that the book is going where it can do the company the greatest good.

My assignment was to write a covering letter to go out with the books. The letter I forwarded to them started with, "You, as a gracious hostess . . ." The balance of the letter played on her vanity, her natural desire to be admired by her family and friends, the important role the company's products could play in achieving that ambition, and where she could buy the products. And, of course, she was thanked for requesting the book.

Back came the letter from the client. This wasn't the type of letter he wanted at all. He saw no point in using up so much space in thanking her and in flattering her. "We've already got her half dollar!"

Keep your eyes on the target. This man had the mistaken notion that the purpose of his magazine advertising was to sell books at fifty cents each and that the selling of his merchandise represented a fresh, new effort. Of course, that wasn't the case. The selling of his products *started* with the magazine ad. When a prospect mailed a request for the book, accompanied by payment, he had his selling foot in the door. The book and the accompanying letter amounted to the sales presentation, leading up to the all important close, when the prospect goes to the store and makes the purchase. And that last step *is* the target.

If a good salesperson had called on whoever requested the book, he or she would have been the substitute for the covering letter. You can easily see him or her, smiling in a friendly manner, saying agreeable things that would win the prospect's friendship and trust. The function of the letter is no different.

A letter with a give-away is the salesperson. Many people ask "Why bother with a covering letter?" They argue that the book is what was requested. The book does a good selling job of the product—or it should. The book tells where and how to buy the products. The covering letter, they reason, is a needless extra expense.

Testing has proven that the covering letter can add greatly to the eventual good results. The main thing the letter does is to add the personal element. The book was printed for mass distribution. Nothing personal there. The letter is a *private message to one individual from another*. That, in itself, is flattering. The book speaks of a number of things. The good covering letter serves to focus attention on the few things of vital importance to the advertiser.

Form letters can be personal. Form letters have been referred to in several places throughout this book. You have seen that even though they *are* form letters, and don't pretend to be anything else, they can succeed in giving the reader the feeling that he or she is being addressed personally.

Here is a letter used by a maker of drapery materials when responding to a request for advertised literature.

Dear Friend:

In reply to your request we are sending you a copy of our booklet, "Bring New Life to Your Windows." This booklet features the story, complete with illustrations, of an old-fashioned house and how it was made to look fresh and modern with exciting window treatments. As you study the details you will be impressed with the important part a few simple and economical ideas played in its modernization.

A Data Sheet is included in this booklet which you may complete and send to us if you have specific window decorating problems. With that information we will be glad to send you, free of charge, detailed color scheme suggestions for the rooms you wish to up-grade.

Enclosed with this letter you will find a list of drapery and curtain specialists in your vicinity who can supply any of the handsome fabrics you will see in our booklet. Rely on their professional guidance for color selection and in the choice of window treatment that will do the most for you.

Thank you for giving us the welcome opportunity to show what we can do to help you to find new joy and pride in your home.

Sincerely,

Let's explore some of the things this well composed letter does. The very first sentence reminds the reader that this is something he or she asked for, and not a blind ad mailed at random. That is an important reminder. It is calculated to insure the reader's full interest. But the writer of this letter knows *people*. The writer knows that the degree of interest that impels you to send for something today may have decreased materially by the time the request has been filled. Two-thirds of the letter, therefore, is devoted to *reselling the value of the give-away*. Your enthusiasm and interest are rekindled.

The final paragraph of the letter spells out how the reader can take action: how to buy their materials locally. It does more than that. It introduces local dealers and sells them.

HAVING THE LOCAL REPRESENTATIVE DELIVER THE REQUIRED ITEM

Some advertisers, under some circumstances, have a slightly different target when they offer a booklet or premium in their advertising. They want to get their salespeople into the homes or offices of the people who inquire. The give-away is the salesperson's pass.

The advertiser realizes, however, that some people don't like a salesperson to call. A certain amount of resistance exists. To pave the way for the salesperson's call, a letter can melt away the resistance. It can, in any event, reduce it. When you are told that a salesperson will

call, you are less likely to resent their appearance than you might if
they popped in without warning.

One manufacturer of industrial janitor supplies handles inquiries
from business firms in this manner:

Dear Ms. Executive,

Thank you for your recent request for our chart on floor care. This is a
handsome wall chart that's easy to read, handy to use and is all
"meat"—no frills. It's loaded with the sort of information that only a
company like ours, specializing in floor maintenance for more than half a
century, can supply. Our industrial representative in your territory will
be bringing it to you soon. He is:

John Brush

Tall Building

Your Town

But that's not all. He will also give you—yes, give, with absolutely no
strings attached—a gallon can of Floorglow, the magical "once-over"
floor cleaner. We are doing this for just one reason. We want you to
prove to yourself that Floorglow is everything we say it is . . . truly a
miracle product of modern scientific research that will save you time,
money, and labor in floor cleaning. Just follow, the directions on the
wall chart and see if you don't agree.

So keep your eye out for our Mr. Brush. He's got things for you. In the
meantime, the enclosed folder will give you an idea of the important
savings Floorglow will bring you. We're enclosing a miniature of the
Floorglow Chart, too, to serve until you receive your mounted chart for
display.

Once again, many thanks for your interest.

Very truly yours,

The opening uses the same technique we've seen in other types of
replies to give-away requests. There is the reminder that Ms. Executive
mailed an inquiry. She is given a refresher on the values in the
give-away she requested. Then Ms. Executive is told that the chart will
be delivered and by whom.

In the second paragraph Mr. Brush is *sold*. Ms. Executive learns that
she'll get an extra reward for seeing Mr. Brush when he visits her. The
final paragraph reinforces the message that she'll be gaining something
by seeing John Brush and—just in case she's at all unhappy that she
hasn't gotten her wall chart yet—she's told that a miniature of the chart

accompanies the letter. All possible objections have been anticipated and each has been answered in a positive manner.

MAILING THE REQUESTED MATERIAL BUT FOLLOWING-UP WITH A SALESPERSON'S CALL

Some advertisers follow the policy of mailing the requested give-away and then sending one of their salespeople to call on the inquirer. This is a less delicate situation than the one covered by the letter you just read. The salesperson is not tied to the receipt of the gift, but comes later. The fact that you asked for the gift creates a certain amount of moral obligation to receive the salesperson. It is sound, however, to advise the inquirer that the salesperson *will* follow. This is particularly true when dealing with business people.

Some companies handle this situation with great simplicity. When they receive a request for advertised literature, this is the type of covering letter used:

This is the

XYZ LITERATURE

you requested . . .

An XYZ representative will call on you soon to give you complete, on-the-spot information about our complete line of products, and how they can be of help to you.

After the customary reminder that the literature was requested by the prospect the letter briefly, but invitingly speaks of the benefits the salesperson's call offers.

FITTING THE REPLY TO THE PROSPECT

Advertising in publications and over the air will produce a variety of replies. Some are from excellent prospects. Some are questionable, because of the type of company or individual responding or because of geographic considerations. Some are not prospects at all. They are the idly curious, students, or chronic coupon clippers who will send for anything that is free.

It costs a little more to classify your inquiries and handle them differently, but it pays. You have an obligation to send the offered material to all who respond to your invitation. You do not, however, want to encourage the nonprospects to impose upon you further. Some thoughtful advertisers, therefore, go all out with their covering letters to prime prospects, slack up on the questionable inquiries, are polite, but brief with the impossibles.

The DR Group Inc., sales promotion and direct response advertising counsellors of Boston and New York, make public offerings of a booklet called The DR Group: Who We Are, What We Do. This is how they compose their covering letters for the three classifications of inquiries they receive:

Reply to prime prospects.

Dear Mr. Top Asker:

Thank you for requesting a copy of the booklet, which was offered in a recent DR Group advertisement.

Your copy of Who We Are, What We Do is enclosed. We believe you will find this booklet interesting for a number of reasons. In essence, it gives a complete explanation of how the DR Group works and the experience behind this company. Then, it goes on to spell out all the advantages of our services as an adjunct to an inside staff. And, it explains why there is no overlap between the work performed by a general advertising agency . . . shows why you need the counsel of both.

You will read the first part of the booklet with special interest, too. This section covers the basic fundamentals and functions of direct advertising, and may add to your knowledge of what this medium can do. There are observations about the use of direct response advertising as a means of getting sales results up, and selling cost down . . . objectives which are particularly pertinent today.

Naturally, this booklet cannot interpret the value of our services as applied to your business. But personal discussion might very well lead to something that would be beneficial to you and your company.

An invitation from you is all that is necessary—either by letter or telephone. Please feel free to take this step, without the slightest sense of obligation.

> Cordially yours,
>
> The DR Group Inc.
>
> C. James Schaefer
> President

Reply to borderline prospects.

Dear Mr. Questionable Asker:

Thank you for requesting the booklet which was offered in a recent L ... Group advertisement.

Your copy of Who We Are, What We Do is enclosed. This booklet describes the specialized services The DR Group offers in planning, writing, and producing direct response advertising and sales promotion material. It sketches our methods, tells about our three working arrangements, lists the people for whom we work.

Beyond this, you will be interested in the timely observations on the application of direct advertising to the special sales problems of today.

Again—thank you for your interest.

Cordially yours,

The DR Group Inc.

C. James Schaefer
President

Reply to nonprospects.

Thank you

. . . for your recent request for a copy of our booklet, The DR Group: Who We Are, What We Do. We are happy to send you the enclosed copy, and hope you will find it of interest.

Cordially yours,

The DR Group Inc.

C. James Schaefer
President

The first and second letters, processed on fine engraved stationery, are personalized. The third letter is processed on an attractive but inexpensive short letterhead and is not personalized.

The first letter tells a very full value story. It ends up with a request for action. The second letter has less to say and eliminates any action request. The third letter merely thanks the reader for his or her interest.

Perhaps the most significant lesson to be learned from this professional letter writing organization's handling of its own advertising inquiries lies in the fact that they demonstrate their solid belief in the use of a covering letter. *They use one even where they have little or no hope for business.*

The chance of getting a positive response from the inquirers in the third category may be only one in a hundred. The DR Group still feels that since they have invested money in the preparation and mailing of their book, it would be foolhardy not to present the book in the most effective manner possible: by adding the personal touch.

A unique shop specializing in the mail order selling of English Saddlery had an attractive catalog of its products and invited the public to request free copies. When you requested the catalog, here's the letter you would get.

Dear Mrs. N ——————————,

You will receive my 88 page catalog in another envelope.

I think that perhaps the best way to thank you for your inquiry and let you see for yourself the genuine Super Quality of the Saddlery items in my catalog is to make you this—

Special Offer Good For Ten Days Only

On receipt of your first order for any item, I will send you without charge, a large copy 7x10 inches, of the important English Hunting Print on the front of my catalog. It is suitable for framing. You can hang it in your own home or use it as a gift to any sportsman.

This offer holds good regardless of the amount of your order. Should the goods ordered be unsatisfactory in any way, you may return them and the full purchase price will be refunded.

I trust you will accept this limited offer by return mail.

Yours,

The letter precedes the catalog. Because it arrives by itself it is handled a little differently than a letter riding with a catalog. It says little about the coming book. Instead, the letter rolls up its sleeves and starts selling. In Chapter 14 of this book, "How Letters of Reply are Followed-up," you'll see three letters this company used to follow-up each inquiry.

Accredited Mailing Lists, Inc. developed an innovative system they dubbed "List-O-Matic." In media advertising and at trade shows and conventions Accredited offered a booklet explaining the new system. These are the letters they used when they received inquiries:

Dear Direct Marketing Friend,

While you were in New Orleans, busy with sessions, private meetings and sharing experiences and ideas with your peers, you still found time to drop your card into the box at our booth. Thanks for asking for an explanation of our new "List-O-Matic System." The booklet you requested is enclosed.

You are one of the first to learn about what the system is and how it operates. The booklet will tell you about it and will show you the benefits you can enjoy. But the only way you can fully appreciate how really helpful a marketing tool "List-O-Matic" can be is for you to see it in operation.

Drop the enclosed card in the mail now and we'll set up an appointment.

Cordially,

Jordan M. Loewenstein

And for those who responded to media ads:

Here's the booklet you wanted
telling what "List-O-Matic"
can accomplish for you . . .

The booklet explains this innovative system. It tells you how you can have your list needs customized via computer, saving you time, giving you an unusually desirable field of choice and in an exceptionally efficient manner.

But this is something you must see to get the full impact of what it can accomplish for you.

<u>I'm going to bring a computer terminal to your office to demonstrate the advantages you can have at your finger-tips.</u>

All I need is the return of the enclosed card. I'll call you to arrange a time suiting your convenience.

Cordially

Jordan M. Loewenstein

The first of the Accredited letters immediately establishes a personal interest link by its reference to the New Orleans meeting. This is something fresh in the reader's mind and assures interest in the letter. It plays to the reader's ego by stressing the fact that he or she will be one of the first to learn of a new mailing list technique. That is not only ego-building, it is intriguing.

The second letter, after the reminder that this is something that was requested, quickly makes the impulse to return the reply form particularly enticing by dramatizing the fact that a computer terminal will be brought right to the office to demonstrate the advantages of the new system.

THINGS TO BEAR IN MIND WHEN COMPOSING A LETTER IN REPLY TO A REQUEST FOR YOUR GIVE-AWAY OFFERS

1. Keep your eyes on the target. Don't get so enthused about your give-away that you bury the effort to sell your product.

2. Think of your letter as the salesperson handing the giveaway to the prospect.

3. Part of your letter should rekindle enthusiasm for the give-away.

4. Always remind readers that they requested the give-away, or information.

5. If a salesperson will deliver the give-away, your letter can help to pave the way for that call by building up and stressing the benefits the salesperson's visit entails.

6. If the delivery of the give-away is to be followed by a salesperson's call, part of your letter should tell how the reader will benefit by that visit.

7. Fit your reply to your prospect. Your covering letter can make an all-out effort with prime prospects, can help to eliminate the expense of further exchanges with the idly curious.

8. The give-away dictates your letter to a great extent. If it is no more than a door-opener—a good will builder—do not dwell on it. If it is vital to your selling effort, let your letter sell the give-away and call attention to the more important portions.

9. If your letter goes to the reader in advance of the mailed give-away, use it to stimulate happy anticipation, to assure an interested reception.

10. If you have a dramatic way of demonstrating your product, feature the novelty.

11. In all cases, close your letter with a request for action.

14

WHEN YOU ASK
FOR MONEY,
INVOLVEMENT, OR TIME

It was in the midst of the American Cancer Society's annual drive for funds. I was visiting with the head of the local organization in my city. He said, "Ferd, look at what was in with our mail this morning."

What he pushed across the desk to me was a stamped envelope. It was addressed just: CANCER—Washington, D.C." No name or return address appeared. The envelope held a crumpled piece of white paper, a simple engagement ring, a wedding ring, a dollar bill. There was nothing else.

For a stunned few moments I just stared at those stark items. Then I asked if I could use a typewriter. What came out of the typewriter was not written by me. That letter wrote itself.

Earlier I had been told that a mailing made to all of the dentists in the area had brought in donations from just 2 percent of the recipients. My "ring" letter was mailed as a follow-up. It produced contributions from 16 percent of the dentists and has since continued to work its magic with other lists and in other parts of the country.

The letter was run under a photograph of the original envelope and its contents. No letterhead was used. This was the text.

I almost wish we had not been sent one contribution that came in last week's mail. It lives with me. It gives my mind and soul no peace.

The mails were heavy that day. The campaign was under way. There were hundreds of letters . . . donations . . . offers to help . . . appeals for help. And in that great mass of mail there was one envelope . . . a commonplace stamped envelope.

In the envelope was a plain piece of soiled paper. Carefully wrapped in the paper we found . . . a dollar bill, an engagement ring, a wedding ring.

There was no name. No return address. No message. Just those well worn items.

No message?

Yes, there was a message . . . an overwhelming, heart breaking message.

And if the anonymous sender had found it in his heart to put his feelings in words, I can see that message too . . .

"This is all that's left. God spare others from the agony she knew . . . from the anguish I know."

Are you fighting cancer? Have you given?

Enclosed, of course, were a contribution form and reply envelope.

Emotion? Yes, this is a thoroughly emotional approach. There are people who, when planning mail campaigns for gifts to charity, health and similiar causes say, "Let's not get too emotional." They might as well say, "Let's not take in too much money."

Why do people give to causes? Solicitations mailed to one's home or business are very private affairs. Your friends, family, business associates have no knowledge as to what you do. You know. No one else. There is no pressure on you to respond as there is when someone calls on you in person. With outside judgments ruled out, what can exert enough pressure on you, me, or the folks next door, to open our checkbooks and give? Emotion is the inescapable answer.

Did you choke up a little when you read that cancer letter? I wrote it years ago and I still feel its emotional pull every time I reread it. Would logic have changed a 2 percent return to a 16 percent return? Impossible. Only an emotional appeal that carried the ring of truth with it could create such a miracle.

If you are involved with any kind of fund raising by mail, do some digging. Sit down with the people who live with the services rendered . . . whose daily work makes them deeply aware of the need for funds and the deprivations that will ensue if the funding effort falls short of its goals. The facts you will gather can give you dozens of stories that are emotion packed. These should dictate the appeal letters you'll use.

Make your emotional appeal vivid. Were you to talk about the severe plight of hundreds of thousands of people afflicted by a certain disease, and the need to raise money to fight that disease, you might get a relatively fair response. But take a single child, or an old man or woman, and draw your need portrait around the one individual. The results will soar. It is so much easier to communicate a powerful mental image of a person, particularly an appealing person, than it is to try to mentally embrace multitudes of people: masses. The individual is a human factor. Masses are statistics. People give to people, not to statistics.

Nothing about any form of persuasion by mail is absolute. If every mailing asking people to make donations to worthy causes hung its hat on the portrayal of a single person, the effectiveness would become blunted. No single charitable agency can use that approach with all of its appeals for the same reason.

The Columbia Lighthouse for the Blind in Washington, D.C., in the following letter, did not focus on an individual, but did the next best thing. It put the spotlight on a class: little children.

Dear Mr. Jones,

It's easier not to think about them . . .

But there are blind children . . . boys and girls who will never delight in the pure beauty of a flower or the laughter on a friend's face . . . see a TV show or the printed page in a school book.

Only in the past few decades have they had any hope of high achievement. Today there are blind lawyers, teachers, and other professionals. Blind adults hold jobs in industry and work on assembly lines making complex products for diversified companies. Many are employed at Columbia Lighthouse. Such accomplishments were not easily reached. It took years of training and the most successful of these achievers began as children.

That's why the Lighthouse offers a program in which preschoolers learn skills to prepare them for entering classes with sighted children. Viewing them as they play games, mingle with their friends, dress, and feed themselves, it is possible to forget they are blind.

It just so happens they are!

And they need your help and ours. Won't you show you care by sending a generous gift soon?

Sincerely,

P.S. To meet our goal this year we will need many gifts of $25 or more. While we hope you will consider such a gift, all amounts are urgently needed and appreciated.

It isn't difficult to build your own mental pictures while reading that letter, is it? Your emotions are involved and if they are involved sufficiently you'll reach for your checkbook.

Appeals to corporate givers and foundations call for different strategies. The person at a public utility, or a large corporation who decides that the organization should or should not give, and how much, lives in another world. Policy, public relations, responsibility to shareholders are major considerations when they are asked to donate. Not the least of the factors weighed, in many cases, is the question: is it good business?

Appeals addressed to that final question can satisfy all other business criteria.

Here, then, is another Columbia Lighthouse appeal, addressed to such an audience.

Dear Mrs. Keene,

Keeping visually handicapped individuals off the welfare roles and helping them to become tax payers is one of the Lighthouse's most vital activities.

Newly blinded men and women need a vast amount of help and guidance. The huge psychological blow must be overcome. Skilled case workers on our staff go to them and show them and their families that life without vision is, by no means, the end of life.

Next, these unfortunate people come to our wonderful new headquarters building. In particular they come to the "home" within the building. It consists of a living room, kitchen, bedroom, and bath. Here they learn how to return to normal living—how to do for themselves. They are instructed in mobility, indoors and on the streets. And then attention is concentrated on work skills.

The men and women in this program are given back so much of what they thought they had lost. Their hope, their dignity, their means of being independent productive citizens are returned.

Their gains are beyond measure. The community's gains are clear. Your support of this meaningful program is needed now. It's a sound investment.

Sincerely,

This business appeal letter has not been stripped of emotional appeal. People and their tragedies are tellingly present, but practical, logical, believable reasons for giving have been made dominant. This particular mailing was accompanied by a card showing the costs of the various activities mentioned in the letter. The potential givers were shown some big dollar targets they could shoot at.

IN THE POLITICAL WORLD

The knowledgeable use of emotional appeals is not confined to charities, health drives, and similar causes. The lives of politicians can be difficult to the point of plunging them into legal problems and court costs that can lead them to bankruptcy.

What you are going to read is a dramatic example.

A Congressman was subjected to a series of charges that impelled him to fight back. The costs of his battles were overwhelming. He lost everything he had. His only hope of paying off his debts, saving his career, and putting his life back in order was to present his case to people who had supported him in the past. Even there he was blocked by Congressional rules and regulations. He turned to Jim Martin, an Alexandria, Virginia, letter writing consultant who specializes in political campaigns.

Because of the nature of the appeal the identity of the Congressman and his wife are not revealed, but this important fact can be . . . *this letter raised $250,000 net.*

Dear Friend: I'm the wife of a conservative Congressman and I need your help. My family and I are the victims of a long political nightmare and our fight for survival now depends on me. Let me explain why I'm writing this letter to you.

Quite frankly, I'm appealing to your sense of justice and fair play. Here's why.

Three continuous vicious years of personal and political attacks on my husband by powerful liberals and labor bosses have forced us into outrageous expenses and a huge politically caused personal debt.

My husband, Congressman _____, a nationally known conservative leader, has for two straight elections withstood every assault the liberal opposition could muster.

They have charged him wildly and pushed him into investigation after investigation which never proved anything but his honesty. Their ugly attempts even included the use of illegal means to invade our private tax and credit records.

These tactics cost his campaign committee over $400,000 for the past two elections in a state where such races average $75,000 each.

This means our friends and supporters have been forced by dirty tricks and harassment to overspend by a quarter of a million dollars more than we should have needed to win. With great effort most of this campaign money has been raised.

However, the attacks and dirty tricks took their toll personally and we find ourselves faced with a huge politically caused personal debt similar in amount to the campaign expenditures.

My husband planned to solicit funds to pay these politically caused personal debts and he submitted his proposal to the Federal Election Commission which found no objection.

But now he has run into the political double standards of Congress! The new House Ethics Committee arbitrarily says he can't raise such funds even though they are for political reimbursement and not for personal gain!

To show the inconsistency of their reasoning, during the same period while my husband was carefully asking permission, one Democratic Congressman transferred $99,000 from his political campaign fund to his private funds. And another fund-raising activity was going on for another Democratic Congressman, raising $22,500 to build a new wing on his house!

My husband has beaten the attacks by the liberals now for three years. They couldn't destroy him by investigation, and their harassment couldn't keep him from effectively doing his job or prevent his great achievements in the battle to keep our nation strong and free.

This has been accomplished because of my husband's dedication and long hours, and I've helped him by working full time in his office, without pay, I might add.

However, they have wounded us badly financially, and now have succeeded in stopping him personally from any financial repair, short of resigning from Congress. This is what the liberals want, of course. If they can't defeat you at the polls, it seems they won't quit until they ruin you financially.

Well, they haven't won this battle because I have some rights, too.

Those chivalrous liberals on the House Ethics Committee who are always talking women's rights have just tried to sentence me as a wife and mother of five to an impossible debt burden. But they're not going to get away with it!

My husband is abiding by the decision of the Committee—the so-called Club rules. However, I am not a member of Congress and I am not bound by them.

I am liable for half of my husband's debts and if he should die, I'll have the full burden.

So here's what I've decided. He and I have arrived at a legal and equal division of property and indebtedness where he has assumed the debts of the family, the house, the cars, the charge cards, and so forth, which he will pay properly from his pay check.

And I have assumed a substantial portion of those debts arising from the political dirty tricks—debts of hundreds of thousands of dollars—and urgently ask your help to save my family from financial disaster.

Our three-year battle for survival against the horrors of the liberal harassment will all be for nothing unless I can win this final battle, which I have been forced to do by myself.

Please note. I am abiding by the guidelines of my husband's agreement with the FEC—no funds from corporations will be accepted, nor from federal employees, nor in gifts of $100 or more from one person.

I urgently need your help. The burden on us has been unbelievable. Won't you help me by sending as much as you possibly can, $99, or $75, or even $50, $25, or $10?

I promise you that I will deposit your donation promptly into a special bank account I've set up to pay off these debts.

I anxiously await your reply as soon as possible.

Gratefully yours,

P.S. I'm sending you copies of some of the clippings regarding our situations.

Asking for financial backing. Have you ever received a letter from a candidate for office that was brief? They are exceedingly rare. Experience has shown that those people who are at all likely to donate to a politician's campaign have a thirst for facts. They want to know where the candidate stands on issues. They want to know how he or she has voted in the past and a good deal more.

Martin Advertising Agency was given the challenge to compose a letter that would raise campaign support money from a small group of people who previously had made contributions.

The technique employed was to present an impressive series of facts but in as intimate and friendly a manner as possible. The final effort involved a four page single spaced letter. It was personalized. It was mailed to the home address of each person on the list. It carried an enclosure . . . an 8x10 inch full color photograph of the candidate and his attractive family, hand-inscribed with a message to each recipient. It announced that an autographed copy of a book authored by the candidate was on its way.

Here are the first and last parts of the letter:

Dear Mr. & Mrs. Josephs,

I'm setting aside this time today to write to you and several of my other close friends and supporters to ask for your help.

There is so much to fill you in on that I wish I could meet with you personally.

The movement to restore economic incentives and encourage capital formation has made tremendous progress. My Tax Reduction Bill is now a household word and, in reality, an international cause.

But since we unfortunately can't sit down and talk one-on-one, I hope you'll find time to read my new book. If you haven't already received one, an autographed copy is in the mail and should arrive within a few weeks.

It is really a revolutionary statement, because of its bold implications for getting our free enterprise system moving again. It says, in popular language, the message you and I have been spreading for years:

That we need to restore the American incentive to work, save, and invest by reducing tax rates on both labor and capital.

That we need to elect legislators who are concerned with capital formation and the "supply side" of the economy.

That we need to urge legislators to consider the economic impact of excessive regulation, which acts as a $100 billion a year tax on the time and resources of Americans.

That we need to help policymakers understand that the cause of inflation is not businesses earning profits or workers earning wages. It is the devaluation of our money standard—the dollar—which began in 1971.

Let me also give you some important details that further the idea of incentives and capital formation.

I'm sure you agree that the words, "rebuilding incentive" really . . . .

[This is followed by two full pages of issues and facts, and then . . .]

1980 political primaries begin in just seven months.

I don't need to tell you that campaigns are lost by candidates and committees that wait until 2 or 3 months before an election to begin campaigning and raising funds.

That's why our Committee is starting right now to raise $100,000 for the 1980 primaries and general elections.

I know $100,000 is a lot of money. But that's what is necessary to elect and reelect proponents in all 50 States.

Obviously, I'm going to need your help to meet this fundraising goal of $100,000.

I'm asking, if it's at all possible, for you to send $1,000 or perhaps as much as $1,500 to our Committee. Some of my supporters have already sent the maximum $5,000, though I realize even $1,000 or $1,500 is a lot of money.

But I need your help to keep the momentum going. It's very important that I get your response as soon as possible. So please write me at my home address using the stamped reply envelope.

You can be sure that every dollar of support will go to campaigns that will make a real difference on election day.

But with only seven months until the first primary, it's imperative that I know whether I can count on your financial support.

What's the alternative? With the current recession and with inflation raging out of control, we need new answers to our economic problems based on production and investment, not policies of austerity and "steady as you go."

With your help, we can provide those fresh alternatives. But I must hear from you soon.

The key to victory is your helping us now to keep the movement going full speed through the 1980 elections.

Whatever you can send, you know it will go a long way toward helping not only the Committee, but me personally as I try to promote "the cause" that we both believe in. I know I can count on you.

Sincerely,

P.S. Mr. & Mrs. Josephs, I think of you as part of our inner circle of supporters. As a small way of reminding you that you are part of my larger family of support, I have enclosed an autographed photo.

(The full-color photograph, showing the candidate, his wife, and their smiling children, with the Capitol Building in the background, carried this hand written inscription: "To the Josephs—Without your help things like this wouldn't be happening. Thanks.")

The total cost of this very limited mailing was $700. It brought in $45,700 in donations.

Just look at the amount of "act now" momentum that was built into the latter part of this powerful appeal. Jim Martin did not leave it to the reader to reach his or her own conclusions about the amount of money involved, about the possible size of a contemplated contribution. He came right out and made very positive suggestions, taking no chances that the readers might think small.

The time factor is hit over and over . . . `` . . . primaries begin in just seven months,'' `` . . . campaigns are lost by candidates and committees that wait . . . ,'' ``That's why our Committee is starting right now . . . ,'' ``It's very important that I get your response as soon as possible,'' ``With only seven months until the first primary, it's imperative that I know . . . ,'' ``I must hear from you soon.''

Clearly, professional fund-raiser Jim Martin believes that the need to persuade readers to take instant action is crucial to a successful campaign.

ASSOCIATIONS, CLUBS, AND OTHER MEMBERSHIP ORGANIZATIONS

Associations, clubs, and other types of membership organizations have specialized needs to persuade by mail. They solicit memberships, membership renewal, and attendance at conventions and meetings.

There are two sources of fully professional information about how the mail is used most productively in these realms. One is the American Society of Association Executives (ASAE) and the other is William Dalton, a past president of the ASAE and chairman of the Dalton Group, Inc., a professional consultant for trade and professional associations, operating out of Washington, D.C.

Both Bill Dalton and the ASAE have generously shared their expertise and their experience by providing the material that follows.

Conventions and meetings. Bill Dalton states that communications is 90 percent of an organization's growth and success. ``Conventions and meetings are a vital factor in that 90 percent bracket,'' he says, ``representing the difference between success and mediocrity.''

An organization's publications may play an important role in the promotion of attendance at its conventions and meetings, but the most positive tool for building attendance is the mailings that tell the story, present the benefits, give the members the instruments to enroll, to make hotel reservations, and to take whatever other steps are required.

An ASAE publication, *Making Your Convention More Effective*, copyrighted in 1979, has this to say about selecting the theme:

A theme can do for a convention what the title or theme music does for a play, a motion picture, or a radio or television series. It ties it together, aids identification and recall, creates moods and excitement, dramatizes, and most importantly helps in furthering the objectives of the convention. Some associations have placed even more emphasis on the use of themes by making the convention theme the theme for the association's programs for the year.

1. Does it instantly reflect one of the major concerns or problems facing the membership?
2. Does it serve as a subject matter umbrella under which the majority of program material (at least 75 – 85%) can be encompassed?
3. Does it lend itself to inclusion in the material or comments offered by speakers and other program participants?
4. Does it lend itself to an eye-catching and mind-catching design for a convention logo?
5. Does it lend itself to "dramatization?"
6. Is it a catch phrase that will permeate conversations at the convention?
7. Will it likely become such a catch phrase that members will use it after they return home from the convention?
8. Is it provocative?
9. Does it embody more than one element?
10. Does it suggest either a personal or tangible goal?
11. Is it honestly not trite and in keeping with the dignity of the audience?
12. Does it stimulate imagination?
13. Will it suggest action?

Turning to the actual development of the direct mail promotion of a convention, the booklet makes these points:

Continuity. "If direct mail is the principal effort, too few attempts to sell the prospect can actually be a waste of effort and money. The sixth or seventh mailing may be the one that makes the sale."

"Seven seems to be the magic number."

"Start about six months before the convention. Space mailings closer together as the convention gets nearer."

Importance of the envelope. The pros and cons of bulk rate as opposed to first class postage are discussed and it is pointed out that a study revealed that about 10 percent of bulk rate mail is lost and another 10 percent is never opened. You must make the decision as to whether this 20 percent loss in readership is or is not a fair price to pay for the difference in postage cost. What is not mentioned in this discussion, but is worthy of consideration, is what percentage of a first class mailing might get tossed out without being read.

The great value of attractive teaser copy on the mailing envelope is covered in this article. Well-conceived, they can be almost irresistible forces. They impel people to open envelopes and read what they carry. The booklet offers a few fine examples including these gems:

"Convention Discount Information Inside"

"Your ticket to the XYZ reception enclosed"

Bear in mind that the name of the association also appears on the envelopes. Those teasers are addressed to people who are interested, dues-paying members.

Writing the letter. While the greater part of this discussion includes points covered and illustrated in other parts of this book, of special importance is the advice that you write nothing until you are thoroughly familiar with the convention program. The subjects to be covered, the qualifications of speakers and panel members, the color and excitement of social and special events, are the things you must know if you are going to promote properly the things the reader will gain by saying YES.

The samples of convention and meeting letters that follow were supplied by Bill Dalton as typical examples of effective attendance building mailings.

AMERICAN TRUCKING ASSOCIATION
Sales and Marketing Division

Ladies and Gentlemen:

The Annual Meeting of the Sales & Marketing Council, American Trucking Associations, Inc., will be held at the Del Monte Hyatt, Monterey, California, Sunday, April 27 through Wednesday, April 30.

This first mailing includes the initial Member Technical Program, hotel reservation form (which must be received by the Del Monte Hyatt by March 20), and other related inserts. A Fact Sheet containing info on transportation to the hotel, weather, etc., will be in future mailings.

In accordance with our By-Laws, the membership of the Council shall be made aware of any proposed By-Laws changes ten (10) days prior to this meeting and the registrants at the Annual Meeting shall vote on same.

Use "Forward Vision in the Decade Ahead," plan on attending this Annual Meeting. Register today. I look forward to seeing you in April.

Sincerely,

The effectiveness of this extremely down-to-earth, businesslike letter is that it conveys the writer's conviction that the recipients will attend. That feeling is powerfully projected by its directness, by the total lack of promotional copy. The reader's natural impulse is to turn to the enclosures for a serious consideration of participating.

Nothing has been said or done in this first in a series mailing to give a reader cause to throw up any mental roadblocks. There is nothing to resist for there is no apparent sales effort.

The theme is utilized and the member is given reason to act at once.

The strength of a series of letters is that you can start low key, knowing that the opportunities to increase the excitement and the pressure are in your hands.

The biggest, boldest type on the letter that follows is:

SAN FRANCISCO—Everybody's Favorite City

NATIONAL BEER WHOLESALERS ASSOCIATION

Dear NBWA Member:

Enclosed is advance information for the NBWA Spring Meeting being held in San Francisco, May 8–12.

Work is going on to put together a program keyed to day-to-day concerns of NBWA members with emphasis on current items of importance in the industry. A brief outline of the schedule for the meeting is included in this brochure for your planning convenience. As the plans for the business and social programs are developed, more information will be sent to you.

Please read the enclosures carefully and return the indicated forms as soon as possible to be assured of accommodations you prefer. The Hotel St. Francis has been selected as the site for our meeting. This San Francisco landmark is one of the premier hotels in the country and offers fine meeting facilities combined with superb guest accommodations.

A preconvention wine tour is being arranged for May 6–8 and a postconvention industry tour to New Zealand and Australia will depart San Francisco on May 12.

We hope attendance at the convention will benefit every participant. We invite you to join us in San Francisco and we encourage registration of other members of your organization.

[Hand signed by both the NBAW President and Convention Chairman]

When writing promotional letters intended to entice lots of people to come to a convention, be aware that you are addressing two audiences.

You are talking to the man or woman who may want to attend and you are also talking to the executive who will be asked if they *may* attend. The individuals who will be interested in taking the trip are very susceptible to where the convention will take place, how good the accommodations will be, the social events, the spouses' program, and other alluring elements. They may also be attracted by what they can learn, what contacts they may make, and steps they might be able to take to advance the interests of their companies. But everyone is human and even the owners and heads of companies who are invited to attend are subject to the romance aspects of your promotion.

Be sure that your mailings help those people who must get a higher up's okay. Don't let your literature make the social side so dominant that you weaken their ability to say, ''I think it is good business for me to be there.''

The NBWA letter steers a wise middle course. The first half of the letter talks almost pure business, a program enclosed with the letter is referred to. The brochure's almost total stress is on the specific topics that will be addressed, the industry leaders who will let down their hair (if any) and tell how they are solving common problems.

And, by no means is the romancing overlooked. The lure of San Francisco, the space given to the great hotel and its luxurious accommodations, the wine tour, and the post convention trip to New Zealand and Australia, add up to heady attractions.

The desirable accommodation angle is employed to urge prompt action. ''Move now and nail down one of the better rooms in the best hotel'' is a great act-now motivator. Finally, this smartly composed letter suggests that the member addressed consider bringing along others in the organization who might benefit from being there.

Selling convention exhibitors can be the answer as to the profitability of a convention.

THE TENNESSEE SOCIETY OF ARCHITECTS

Dear Ms. Phillips,

Planning for the second Annual Tennessee Society of Architects Convention and Building Products Exposition is in high gear. I can promise you one of the most stimulating, thought-provoking conventions in the Society's history.

This year's session will be held at the beautiful Sheraton Nashville Motor Inn, September 3 – 5. Exhibitors will appreciate the convenience of having all activities on one floor level.

This annual exposition provides exhibitors an opportunity to show their latest products, equipment, and services to the largest gathering of architects, specification writers, and designers in the state.

As in the past, space will be assigned in accordance with the priority system outlined in the rules section of this brochure. I cannot urge you too strongly to make early application for the space your company desires.

I invite you to participate in this hospitable architectural convention.

Sincerely,

The Tennessee Society of Architects' letter to potential space buyers wraps up three attractions in one letter. They open their letter by addressing the recipients as they would their own members. The emphasis is on program. Exhibitors and their staff, attending convention sessions, do have the beneficial opportunity to broaden their knowledge of the needs and desires of their customers: the architects. Next, they are told of the attractiveness of the facility and the absence of the one thing exhibitors dread, having the exhibit area located where it is inconvenient for the members to visit: ". . . all activities on one floor level."

Reason to make an affirmative decision, and to do so at once, is believable and strong. Location is immensely important to exhibitors.

An interesting word appears in the final paragraph: hospitable. What an inviting image that creates. It says that the members attending the exhibit area will welcome their presence, will view their offerings in an open, friendly manner. A fine letter.

GETTING AND KEEPING MEMBERS

Using the mails to sell organizations and individuals to join organizations is not vastly different from other mail sales efforts. You are offering benefits. The benefits cover such attractions as increased profits, ways of solving problems common within an industry or profession, keeping up-to-date on legislation, innovation, competition, opportunity, personalities, and kindred matters, and a great deal more. Not least of the attractions membership encompasses is the matter of prestige: the right to put a plaque on your wall, a line on your letterhead and business card, a legend in your ads saying that you belong.

These are just some of the surface plusses a membership campaign can hold forth. One of the things that makes the mail selling of memberships a bit less of a problem than most other types of direct mail is that your audience is readily identified. Every piece you spend money on will go directly to a genuine prospect. That is an "upper" and, at the same time, it may be a "downer." The fact that it is so easy to isolate every potential member also means that every previous effort you, or others, have made to increase membership have gone to the same people.

You face a challenge, therefore, to create mailings capable of breaking through the unspoken barricade of, "I've seen that before. I know what they say. I'm not interested." Your mailings have to be better than the ones that went before.

There are vast differences betwen the letters that will solicit membership in a professional association, for example, and ones that offer memberships in more mundane trade associations.

Here, for example, is a sparkling letter taken from ASAE's Membership Director's Manual, copyrighted in 1976. The letter was written on the letterhead of the Best Linen Supply Company of Indianapolis.

Dear Fellow Linen Supplier,

I'm George Pattison, a linen supplier here in Indianapolis. I have been operating the Best Linen Supply Company for 20 years and I've got four routes. I'm a member of the Linen Supply Association of America. In fact, I'm an enthusiastic member. Enthusiastic enough to write this letter to you, suggesting that it's good business to be in the National Association. I find it so and I don't think I'm much different from you.

I can't afford a production engineer to show me how to cut my operating costs. And I can't pay a high grade lawyer to keep me up to date on the many Washington laws that I have got to know about—if I expect to stay in business.

How can I get the services of an expert sales consultant? I can't afford to put on a big advertising campaign to push linen supply. Nor can I develop sales manuals for my routemen, training films for my few employees, special films for the public so that they'll have more respect for my business.

All these expensive and valuable services, and many more, are what I get as a member of the National Association. It's almost unbelievable that for the $100 a year I pay in dues, I can get expert advice on so many important subjects and the right kind of leadership for our industry. By putting our money and efforts together, you and I get our investment back hundreds of times over.

I'm in the National Association because I get a great deal of good from it. I ask you to join because I know that the bigger the association is, the more it can do for me and my industry. Come on in.

Sincerely yours,

George H. Pattison

With natural ease, the benefit story comes through resoundingly. The technique of having a real live member telling a fellow plant owner what the association gives him is strong medicine. Writing a letter of that type forces you to be conversational, practical, clear, and compelling.

In contrast, Bill Dalton offers another type of membership letter. This one is addressed to professionals; potential members of the Society of Plastic Engineers. The tone and the reasons why change radically.

Dear Mr. Doe:

SPE publications, meetings and related activities—and the close personal contacts you will develop among your fellow XYZ Section members—can provide valuable information and ideas . . . often before they become generally known.

As the enclosed brochure explains, SPE membership offers you these and many other worthwhile benefits and privileges—all aimed at furthering your professional growth.

Participation in a Society, which enjoys a worldwide reputation, is a most effective way to enhance your own professional prestige.

Note, particularly, that in addition to the SPE national and regional conferences, you will have an opportunity to participate in Divisions designed to meet your special needs, and to join in the activities of our Section. This brings the benefits of SPE membership "close to home," enabling you to make the most of your membership.

If you feel, as we do, that you may qualify for SPE membership, we cordially invite you to complete the accompanying application and send it to us in the postage-paid envelope enclosed. You can be assured that we are looking forward with pleasure to welcoming you as a member of the Section and the Society.

Sincerely,

Don't let them get away. The costs of winning new members is far too great simply to hope that their affiliation will continue. You retain members by keeping all of your campaign promises, and a little bit more. You constantly remind them of the value of the benefits membership entails. You relentlessly follow-through when renewal time comes and the dues bill is not honored.

Welcome new members. Get new members started on the right foot by letting them know that you are aware of their enrollment and reinforcing their decision to join. And, by all means, do it at once.

Bill Dalton submits this as a good example of a welcoming letter.

NATIONAL INSTITUTE OF REAL ESTATE BROKERS

Dear New NIREB Member:

Your application in the National Institute of Real Estate Brokers has been processed and it is a pleasure to include you as a member of the Institute.

Your membership in the division (s) will be of much benefit to you in the years to come. Membership unites leading specialists from across the country with each participating on an individual level within his particular areas of interest or expertise. It is this participation which has motivated the Institute to be creatively unique in the industry.

So that you can better get to know the work of the Institute and those people most actively involved, I would sincerely urge you to take part in the affairs of NIREB. As a member, you are welcome to participate to the fullest extent in all educational programs. Through this observation and acquaintanceship, you may judge how your Institute will best serve you and how you may best serve your Institute.

To insure our accuracy in having the services reach you, would you kindly fill out the appropriate spaces on the enclosed card and drop it in the mail to us? Thus we will be certain of your address, spelling of name, and that you receive your services on schedule. Thank you.

Be watching for your membership services which should begin to arrive within the next few weeks. And may I close with these words: read what you receive from your Institute, and then put what you learn to use in your business life. I promise that you will realize a great return from your investment.

Sincerely,

When the dues are not paid, it does not mean that the member has decided to drop out. In many cases it is nothing more than an oversight, red tape, or plain procrastination. Well-planned letters can correct such causes. At the same time the letters must address themselves to the possibility that the fires need rekindling. It is so easy to permit a series of membership services to become routine, accepted as normal events, that the underlying practical values become submerged. If the renewal bill arrives at belt tightening time, it presents itself as an easy, quick way of cutting costs. Your renewal letters, therefore, must restate benefits in ways that bring the values back to the surface.

There comes a time, however, when it becomes evident that some stronger persuasive tactics are needed. From Bill Dalton's files here are two good examples of how to raise the renewal temperature without becoming offensive.

AMERICAN SOCIETY OF ASSOCIATION EXECUTIVES

Dear Mr. Layback:

LET'S TALK SHOP! You have been a valued member of the American Society of Association Executives, but for some reason you have not renewed your membership. Frankly, I don't know why— SO I'M ASKING!

By remaining inactive this coming year, you're going to miss the many benefits that include the monthly Association Management magazine, special report on government relations activities, professional development and educational programs, the ASAE Annual Convention, the ASAE Gold Card, and so much more.

These ASAE benefits translate into important administrative tools that help you direct the affairs of your association. That's the reason every year over 6,000 executives, like yourself, renew and remain active in ASAE.

Most often we find that association executives are extremely busy people. In many cases, they don't know that their membership has lapsed. This may be the reason you have not renewed.

Whatever the reason, we lost you and we want you back. And if there is some way we can improve our service, we would like to know that too. Good news or bad news—we want to know.

The key to any well managed membership program is knowing what's on the member's mind. Please take a moment and tell me. I've enclosed a HINT-O-GRAM for you. ASAE is paying the postage for your reply—so we are serious.

As you complete the Hint-O-Gram, consider the advantages of membership in ASAE. For only a few dollars a month, billed annually, you receive essential information, knowledge that will assist you and perhaps save your association thousands of dollars. That's a bargain.

So when you finish this letter and while it's fresh in your mind fill out the Hint-O-Gram. Tell us what you would like to see from us and please renew your membership in ASAE.

Sincerely,

Dear Past Member:

Every man owes a part of his time and money to the business or industry in which he is engaged. No man has a moral right to withhold his support from an organization that is striving to improve conditions within his sphere. —Theodore Roosevelt

Could SPE strive to improve conditions within your sphere? The answer is "yes." The Society attempts to improve the aura of plastics information within technical areas in which members work. This it does through publishing the SPE journal, Polymer Engineering and Science, SPE technical volumes and conducting regional and national technical conferences.

Of course you could subscribe to, or attend, all of these Society projects without becoming a member. And maybe you do, although the extra cost to you would more than pay your membership dues.

But that's not our point. Here we are discussing involvement.

If SPE is to strive harder to improve your conditions, then shouldn't you contribute also by rejoining the Society: Increased membership supplies the wherewithal for SPE to strive harder . . . to better equip you with the wherewithal to better direct your career.

Already many plastics engineers have become specialists. Many more will be doing so. If you are one, then SPE publications and conferences will keep you in touch with the many plastics developments which may relate to your field. Also, the newly formed Divisions are starting to generate specialized newsletters, one or more of which could be of benefit to you.

If you are not a specialist now, the relentless pace of plastics progress will make you one. <u>Now</u> is the time to follow significant developments so that you can direct your career toward a rewarding specialty.

Isn't it to your best interest to <u>rejoin SPE</u>?

Reinstated members now pay no back dues, no initiation fee, just the annual $25 membership dues . . . and are asked to update their applications. If yours doesn't need updating, just tell us so.

Cordially,

MAIN CONSIDERATIONS WHEN YOU ASK FOR MONEY, INVOLVEMENT, OR TIME

1. When seeking public donations to a charity, appeal to the emotions.

2. But if you address corporate or foundation givers, logic and a businesslike approach are vital.

3. Emotional appeal letters are most effective if they portray the plight or needs of a single individual.

4. Emotion can play an important role in some political fund-raising appeals.

5. When seeking support for elective office, the more personal the approach, the more effective it can be.

6. When attracting people to a convention, a colorful theme can be an important help.

7. The first in a series of convention attendance mailings will do well if the writer assumes that the reader will attend.

8. Convention letters must sell the potential attendee plus any higher-up who must okay the trip.

9. Sales letters to potential convention exhibitors should sell the marketing aspect, the convention program, the warmth with which exhibitors will be treated.

10. Membership campaign letters taking the form of testimonials from people in the same business or profession are most effective.

11. Invitations to join a professional association should be composed with a professional tone.

12. Immediately welcome a new association member, reinforcing the benefits of services to be rendered.

13. The effort to renew membership when annual dues will become payable is immensely important, should start early, and involve no less than three mailings, if needed.

15

FOLLOWING THROUGH

Many types of letters require additional letters from you. The reply to a letter of inquiry about a product or service cannot stand on its paper feet unsupported. The support it demands is more letters from you.

People are lazy. Your first response may win interest. It may even win enthusiasm. That's no guarantee that people will act. There is always the urge to put your letter aside with the good intention of *doing something about it sometime.* Sometime rarely comes. Too many other things come along and your letter is forgotten.

People hang back. Your letter giving readers the facts requested may be beautifully written and compelling, but there may be some lingering doubts and fears. This is particularly true when no salesperson or demonstration is involved: when the order must be closed by mail.

People expect further persuasion. Follow-up letters have become such an accepted practice in mail-order selling that people *anticipate* more letters from you. Knowing that they'll hear from you again gives them additional reason for failing to take action *now*.

All of these factors make the follow-up imperative.

You may reason that the person who bothers to mail a letter, card, or coupon of inquiry has demonstrated active interest and therefore a single, well handled reply is enough. It isn't so. If the inquiry were to be handled by a salesperson making a *personal* call you would not expect the salesperson to come back with an armful of orders. You would appreciate the need for the salesperson to make several calls, in many cases, before succeeding. *You can't expect more from paper and ink.* You have every reason to expect less.

The follow-up is essential. It calls for as much thought and attention as your original letter of reply. Perhaps, because you have encountered some indication of resistance, it calls for even more skill.

NRI, in Washington, D.C., is one of the nation's great home study schools specializing in the offering of courses in Television—Audio. Harry Bennett, Director of Advertising for the school, places display ads in many publications. The ads invite readers to send for a free book about opportunities in the communications and servicing fields and for full information about the courses offered.

When an inquiry is received Mr. Bennett sends letters to that person *once a month for five years before he gives up.* That is not a misprint. It is not an exaggeration. *Five years.*

This long series of letters is employed—not because Mr. Bennett is stubborn—but because *he knows that it pays to follow-up that often.* His carefully compiled records tell him so.

This is *not* a rare and exceptional case. Many mail-order sellers have kept the same kind of records and have come to the same conclusions.

NRI follow-up letters differ in appearance, in color, and in size. This is done so that the prospect will not get the mistaken impression that he has received any of the letters before.

Here is a typical follow-up letter used by NRI.

Dear Friend:

Are these three questions bothering you—causing you to delay enrolling:

1. Is there good money to be made in Television—Audio servicing NOW?
2. Does the Television—Audio industry offer a future?
3. Can I make good in Television—Audio?

Let's discuss the questions separately.
1. "Is there good money to be made in Television—Audio servicing NOW?" My answer is yes—and here are reasons for my answer:
Today there is more Television—Audio equipment in use than ever before in history—Broadcasting Stations, Public Address Systems, Aircraft Stations, Police Radio Stations, Home and Auto Radios, FM Receivers, Television Receivers, etc. The men who can make, sell,

install, and service this equipment are finding good jobs at good pay. There's room for many more well trained men in this work.

The National Defense Program, no matter how world conditions may change from month to month, can only increase the need for trained technicians. Manufacturers of Audio and Electronic equipment will need more men than ever before. The military services need technicians.

2. "Does the Television−Audio industry offer a future?"

Let me answer that question by asking if you have read any of the recent magazine and newspaper articles on what's ahead in Audio and in Television? I feel sure you have. Television is a dynamic growth industry and there has been a booming rebirth of Radio broadcasting.

Every recognized authority with whom I have talked—or whose opinion I have read—agrees that all branches of the Television−Audio industry are going forward rapidly to new heights of prosperity . . . and will offer more opportunities to more qualified men than ever before!

3. "Can I make good in Television−Audio servicing?"

Let a few NRI graduates answer this question:

David McMillan, Burnaby, B.C.,Canada

"The Master Course in Color Television Servicing has really helped me to acquire a real working and technical knowledge of TV Servicing. As a matter of fact the course trained me so well that I was able to take over an established TV repair shop the first of July at which time I had still not completed my course. The business is a one man operation but is well known in the area and there is always something to repair. Because of my fine NRI training there has been very little I have not been able to repair. By applying my NRI training to the business I can make a success of it."

Gary Flatt, Pasadena, California

"The benefits of the NRI Television−Audio Servicing Course have been many for me. I have worked some part time and have earned extra money in my spare time. I found the course educational and enjoyable and feel it was inexpensive for what I have already gained from it. I would feel quite confident in recommending NRI training to someone whose goal would be to have a full time business. My NRI Course has been a very interesting and worthwhile experience."

I have room for just one more letter, so I'll quote part of this one from Kenneth C. Collenborne, Big Timer, Montana.

"When I enrolled with NRI, I had a full time job. I was

considering TV repair as an additional part-time job and planned to go into it full-time after retirement from my regular job. As things turned out, I lost my job unexpectedly. Fortunately, I was nearly finished with my NRI course so I was able to set up a full time TV Servicing business. In a short time I was back to work—my own business—my own boss—and no more unexpected lay-offs. For this reason, I would recommend an NRI Course to anyone regardless of their current employment situation.''

Is there any reason why you can't do as well as these fellows . . . or better? Television—Audio offers more opportunities than it did when these men enrolled.

There is money to be made in Television—Audio servicing NOW. The industry does offer you a prosperous, secure future. And I certainly believe you have it in you to make good in Television—Audio.

The main thing standing in the way of your success in Television—Audio servicing is the matter of getting started. Enroll NOW. Get ready to join the ranks of successful, prosperous NRI people.

Sincerely yours,

John F. Thompson
President

NOTE TO VETERANS: NRI Courses are available under all "GI Bills" to qualified veterans. Write me for official forms and special information.

This carefully planned letter attempts to fathom the doubts in the prospect's mind. It takes up some of the reasons why people will delay and hold back. It answers each with powerful logic. It's a long letter, but the writing is vigorous and interesting, carrying the reader along to the end.

Here are the opening statements used in other letters in NRI's series of follow-ups:

Dear Friend:

You remember me, don't you?

Sometime ago I wrote you about the opportunities for good pay and a bright future in Television—Audio servicing.

About that same time I also wrote Carl Stauth, 417 E. Chestnut St., Corydon, Indiana.

Carl Stauth enrolled. His earnings have jumped. He's happier now, feels more secure about his future . . .

Dear Friend:

I believe you will be interested in this story of two men . . . what they did . . . what happened to them.

John Andrews was "not interested" when I wrote him a letter similar to this one you are now reading.

But A.F. Tomalino, Glendive, Montana, decided to mail the card and find out about my offer.

This happened some years ago when I invited Andrews and Tomalino to send for my free book.

Today, Andrews plods along . . . barely meets expenses.

Tomalino, who decided to find out, now has a fine Audio business of his own, which nets him $850 per month.

It may also pay YOU to mail the card—and find out what Television—Audio servicing offers you . . .

Dear Friend:

If I had received your enrollment this morning . . .

. . . I would be sending your first group of lesson texts instead of this letter—and you would be started toward a good Television—Audio servicing job . . .

Dear Friend:

When someone mentions your name . . .

. . . one year, five years, or ten years from today . . .

. . .will people say: "Oh, a nice enough fellow, but he hasn't what it takes . . . he'll never make a success of anything!" . . .

Dear Friend:

Do you agree with C.E. Corbin, RFD 2, 304, Merced, California?

He says in a letter to me: "The way I see it, you have to make up your mind as to what you want to do, and work for that thing!"

That makes sense, doesn't it? . . .

Not everyone could or should use the same methods. NRI and others in the home study field have good reason to use many follow-up letters and long letters. Most home study courses involve a substantial investment of money, time, and effort. The people who respond to home study advertising may have strong desires to take the courses. The letters and folders they get may increase the desire. But the individual is making a momentous decision when signing the application form and paying the initial fee.

The roadblocks of doubt, fear, and lack of self-confidence must be swept aside. It is no easy task for prospects to remove all of those obstacles even though the temptation is strong. Their minds are full of misgivings. Will the course really give them what they want? Will they have the strength of will to stay with the course for one, two, or three years, doing all of the study and completing all of the assignments? Will they learn as much from home study as from a course conducted in a classroom? Is the end result worth the price asked? Can they afford the payments? Will people laugh at them for taking a correspondence course? How much do they really know about the people offering the course? Is this the right career for them?

Those are just a few of the fears and doubts that plague people.

Experienced people in the home study field understand and appreciate these mental roadblocks. They know that a sale will not be made until those questions are answered. They know that many of the poeple who inquire *want* to sign up and *hope* that the answer to their doubts will be provided. They need and want conviction. They feel let down if the school fails to supply the answer to every doubt.

Long letters and many letters are essential when selling costly intangibles. Go back to the NRI letters. Each one attacks the problem from a different angle. Bear in mind that these are just a few letters out of *sixty*. A tremendous amount of solid thinking and understanding lies behind these letters. The complete series was created to handle *every possible objection and fear* that could be present in the minds of prospects.

Fewer and briefer letters are needed when selling tangibles. The offering of a piece of merchandise that can be fully described and illustrated is far simpler. The prospects have a very clear picture of what they will get for the price asked. The task of decision is much easier.

Follow-up letters offering tangibles must SELL. ''Hard sell'' is a term you'll hear often when mail-order specialists get together.

The meaning of the term is clear: give every word a selling job. The prospect inquired. There is some degree of interest in your goods or services. You've sent the information or the literature requested . . .

now, get in there and *sell*! Overcome normal inertia, the very human inclination to put it off. Move people to make affirmative decisions. Persuade them to act *now*.

In the chapter devoted to getting extra mileage from a give-away offer, you saw a letter from a shop specializing in English sadddlery. As is true of all good direct response practitioners, these folks did not give up quickly, or easily, once a prospect displayed interest. After all, how many prospects are there for English saddlery these days?

The follow-up letters combined benefits, charm, and plenty of good, hard sell. Here are some examples:

Dear Ms. N ——————————,

Here's a sporting proposition!

If you expect to be at home for the next two weeks, I would like to send you, charges prepaid entirely at my risk and expense, one of my Special Super Horse Sheets.

This fine sheet comes in either blue or green and you'll be more than pleased at its attractive appearance. The fine quality fast color twill makes it an excellent value.

It has gold binding all around and two gold surcingles, also open front with strap and buckle. This is one of those dependable well made sheets, properly reinforced in front and back so that it will wear and wear. Size either 72″ or 76″.

Simply write on the back of this letter "Send me the sheet"—state size preferred, and send along store references—and I'll do the rest. If you don't like it, just send it back at my expense, and you'll owe me nothing. If you keep it, I'll simply send my bill—not for eighteen or twenty dollars—but only $14.98.

Remember—it won't cost you one penny unless you agree with me that this is the best value you've ever seen.

P.S. If you prefer a bright red sheet with white trimming, I'll send it for the same low price—$14.98.

Dear Ms. N ——————————,

If you'll just say the word by returning the enclosed card, I'll send you a pair of the grandest electric clippers you ever saw, on approval.

These clippers are "tops" and I wish you could see the enthusiastic letters horsemen are writing me about them.

The sturdy little electric motor runs so quietly you hardly can hear it and the sharp cutting blades trim the horse's fetlocks and ears in a jiffy.

The complete description is printed on the card.

When you've read it, just write your name and address and two store references on the card and mail it to me. I'll send the clippers, right away, on approval.

If you don't like them just send them back at my expense and you won't owe me a cent.

Of course, if you prefer to send cash with your order, I'll refund every penny in case you're not delighted with the clippers.

Just send along the card . . . right now.

Yours,

These are selling letters. Each stresses the company's willingness to refund your purchase price if you aren't happy with the goods. This breeds confidence. Each letter provides a reply card for easy ordering and ends with a strong request for action *now*.

In Chapter 8, "Letters That Win Cooperation," you saw a letter John Nuveen & Company sends to current investors suggesting a way of increasing their tax-free income without investing additional capital. The letter brings in a lot of extra business, but not everyone responds to the first appeal.

This is their follow-up letter:

You are right . . .

extra tax-free income

is appealing, BUT—

The recent letters you and other Nuveen Trust investors have received have pulled some people in two directions.

The idea of adding to that part of your income which is free of federal tax, without increasing your capital investment, would be great if only it didn't mean giving up current income.

It is a dilemma, but for many there is an easy solution.

Help yourself to some of each. A flow of monthly checks may be welcome but your best interests might be served were you to earmark part of that income for today spending and part for future spending. The anticipation of future needs may be the more important aspect . . . or, at least, as important.

Keep in mind that you are in charge. You can tell us to use your tax-free Trust income for automatic reinvestment today and cancel those instructions tomorrow. You can start and stop the compounding of your tax-free income with equal ease and speed.

If you do decide that your future needs may be more important than taking all of your tax-free income now, consider, too, the importance of time. The sooner you send us your instructions the sooner your federally tax-exempt income will increase. An additional instruction form and return envelope are enclosed. Show us how you want your Trust income distributions handled. Put it in the mail today.

Sincerely,

In keeping with the original letter, this one reveals that the company knows its customers and appreciates what they may be thinking. The follow-up does what many second and third efforts can and should do. It presents a fresh viewpoint, addresses itself to a different set of emotions. And notice how it closes by making action easy and urging action now.

Years ago I received a follow-up letter after answering an ad about "mountain honey." I don't know if David J. Johnson of Clarendon, Pennsylvania, who called himself, "That Honey Man" is still in business or not, but his letter was so delightful and intriguing I kept it all these years:

You Can Have
What the Bears Didn't Get!

The Black Bears are simply hell on <u>mountain honey</u>! It's a battle as to who gets it first—me or the bears. Sometimes they win—in fact, they beat me to a frazzle and got most of this year's crop. So I offer you what I got left.

You Can't Fool a Black Bear!

They know good honey—which is why they go after mountain honey. They also know it's good for them. Lord, I don't blame the bears but they do make it hard on a guy who's trying to make a living on mountain honey. Why, one year they done $1,000 damage, besides stealing a lot more of my honey. I sure was hopping mad. The first night five bears—FIVE, mind you—came back at eleven o'clock. I made a racket shooting up in the air and scared them off. I didn't want to hurt any bear. NATURE produced that mountain honey so it belonged to them as much as to me. But since I'm now aiding Nature produce it for me near my place, don't you agree I've the right to protect it?

So I thought of a way . . . a humane way. I put up electric fences around the hives. It is run by batteries, but the current must be kept on 24 hours a day. (Now the bears can look for mountain honey in bee trees elsewhere—they won't starve!) But that won't help on this year's crop, most of which they got. (Next year I'll have a lot more honey unless the bees get tempermental and stage a "sitdown strike.")

NOW DON'T CONFUSE MOUNTAIN HONEY WITH ORDINARY HONEY!

Many folks write to ask why my mountain honey is so different from other honey. It has a tang all its own, which makes it popular with those who like honey. Being a mixture of the nectar from many hardy flowers planted by Mother Nature herself and which thrive in the invigorating air of the mountains, it is a blend man can't imitate. It also contains MINERALS and VITAMINS that other honey-producing flowers just don't have!

Another thing, my honey isn't "processed." It's all mountain honey, simply strained. Nothing added . . . nothing subtracted . . . but full of good taste, nourishment and ENERGY. Yep, you can't fool a black bear when it comes to honey! There is much less mountain honey and it's costlier to produce so you can only rarely buy it in stores. You usually have to seek out an apiarist (I believe that's what a bee farmer like me is called) and one who lives among the mountains, of course.

Doctors—even the cautious American Medical Association itself—endorse honey for health. IT'S EASILY DIGESTIBLE! Contains Vitamin C, seven kinds of Vitamin B, most of the minerals found in the human body and is also a mild, gentle, unsuspecting laxative. Honey is also a fine BABY FOOD, a grand food for growing children and an energy-building, delightful sweet for adults, without all the harmful effects of regular sugar. Honey may also be used in baking and other cooking instead of sugar. I include tested recipies with each order I fill.

ALL I CAN LET YOU HAVE AT THIS TIME IS A 10-POUND PAIL of my pure, golden tantalizing, mountain honey. It'll cost you $5.89, delivered to your door by Uncle Sam. A millionaire cannot buy better honey than mine from right off the mountain, even if he paid double the price. I'll be much obliged if you'll enclose check with order. I would send C.O.D., if you wish, but then you'd have to pay the carrying and C.O.D charges and the package might come when you're out—or out of change—and the postman won't take your check like I will.

Should you not agree that my mountain honey isn't as delicious as I've claimed, you may return it and get your money back. I can always use it 'cause the bears got so much of my crop. So don't delay, if you want my pure, ambrosia! ("heavenly" is right!) honey that's all honey. When this letter gets mailed to other folks, I'll probably run out of this year's crop anyway . . . except for my reserve of 10 percent I keep for my regular customers' repeat orders. (Gotta take care of them, you know, . . . as I would with you.)

Use the handy order blank and envelope that don't need any postage.
But please order TODAY so I won't have to send your check back with a
"sorry note," I'm already having printed.

Get acquainted with my mountain honey and see what you've been
missing. And once WE get acquainted by mail, I believe you, too, will
be a customer every year.

Sincerely,

THAT HONEY MAN

Here is humor, fascination, irresistible appeal, hard sell, and a
request for action in one, highly palatable package.

KEEP IN MIND WHEN PREPARING FOLLOW-UP LETTERS

1. Until you assemble accurate records, you cannot know how many
   follow-up letters you can use profitably.

2. If you are selling an intangible, don't fear the use of long letters *if
   you have a lot that's worth saying and if it is said interestingly.*

3. When selling tangible products, make your letters briefer and full of
   sell.

4. Subtlety in your follow-up letters can get results in the higher levels
   of selling.

5. When thinking of follow-up letters, think of *customers* as well as
   prospects.

6. Humor can add to the impact of your follow-up letters.

16

HOW AND WHEN TO PUT HUMOR IN YOUR LETTERS

The appropriate and careful use of humor in your letters can give you excellent results. Make people smile as they read and you kindle a feeling of warmth and friendliness about you and your company. When people smile or laugh they feel good. When they feel good they are more inclined to feel optimistic. When they are optimistic they are more likely to say *yes* to whatever you offer.

But humor can be dangerous. If you have no personal contact with your readers, and do not know too much about them, your use of humor may backfire. A reader may be a serious-minded person who feels that humor should play no part in any business letter. You may, unwittingly, run into a situation where the reader regards the subject matter being discussed so very gravely that your use of humor will antagonize. So, watch your step.

Your humor must be appropriate. Don't ever permit your letter to resemble the outmoded back-slapping salesperson who reels off a series of stories just to entertain. If your efforts to promote a smile or a chuckle are not part and parcel of your message, have to be dragged in and have no direct relation to the heart of the matter, leave out. By all means avoid completely the suggestive or off-color story or remark. That is a gamble you never can afford to take. Stay away from jokes about religion and politics unless it is a religious or political cause you are selling.

Model yourself after the reader. If you are responding to a letter written with humor, you are on safe ground if your reply mirrors the writer's light tone. Don't try to go one better. Stay at the same level and *never* permit the reader to be the butt of your shafts of wit.

A mass mailing was made to everyone living in the vicinity of a new branch of a large department store. The mailing invited readers to open charge accounts. But somebody, in preparing the mailing lists, went overboard. You'll see how and why when you read this letter the store received:

> Dear Friends,
>
> I was very pleased to receive your kind invitation to open a charge account with your store.
>
> However, in spite of the fact that I am well-mannered, clean, quiet, and very sociable, I am considered by most people to be canine.
> Therefore, I feel sure it would be better to send the charge card in my mistress' name as she does my shopping for me—flea powder, leash, food, pans, etc. (One must be well equipped and perfectly groomed, you know!)
>
> She has had accounts with several other area stores since 1943. She has been employed since 1943 with the Telephone Company. She owns our home and has well-established credit as far as I know. Her name is Mrs._____ and we live at _____.
>
> If you will let her have a charge account we'll visit your new suburban store to look at Winter Blanket coats, as mine is definitely shabby. I go to all the best places, hotels, etc., and can take revolving doors and elevators without losing my dignity, but I don't like them.
>
> Yours very truly,
>
> [signed with pawprints]
>
> Miss Patti Patches G_____
>
> P.S. Please hide the soap and shampoo the day we come.

And this was the reply written by the store's advertising manager.

> Dear Miss Patti:
>
> When we were addressing our mail, our cocker spaniel was looking over our shoulder. As soon as he saw your name on our list he persuaded us to address you direct.
>
> You know how spaniels are. Especially one by the name of Peter R—No. 11.

Well, we're easily persuaded, especially when it comes to Pete. In his younger days he was buff-colored—with patches of white—but, alas, the years have taken their toll. He now is mostly white, with one eye not so good . . . and a gleam in the other.

We did our best to try to talk him out of it . . . but to no avail. Little did we know that your mistress would read your mail.

You can tell her that, even tho' we'd prefer you for a customer, we have opened an account in the name of:

[name and address of dog's owner]

After all she may have other uses for this account. People need clothes and things for the home, and, if there are children . . . you know how they go through shoes! Not nearly as simple as a dog's life, but I suppose they must have some fun.

We'll be waiting for you at Royal Park real soon . . . about mid-October. If your mistress will loan you the daily newspaper you'll see all the special things we've planned for the opening day . . . and the days to follow..

As to the revolving doors—they're no problem at our new store. We've a ramp system so you can enter on any level without getting snarled up in those swift-moving contraptions. This is really a baby-carriage and wheel chair ramp, but there's no reason why you can't use it.

Thanks a lot for the paw prints. These we are going to preserve. All good wishes.

Cordially,

The reply captured the delightful tone of the original letter. It remained within the bounds set by the original letter. It is intriguingly whimsical without taking any chance of giving offense. The reader could not help but feel, "Those must be mighty nice, friendly people. I'll enjoy dealing there."

The letter that follows was addressed to the Chairman of the Board of a major appliance manufacturer. The copy you will read has been subjected to a bit of editorial censorship. It's a rare and amazing letter . . . but enjoy it for yourself:

Dear Sir:

Somewhere around the 10th of July, I wrote a letter to your company asking them to send me a new rubber door gasket for the 8-foot kerosene refrigerator that I purchased last fall in Miami, from Mike's Service Station. This Mike Horn might not be your regular dealer in that district, but he at least had a dozen or more of your products in his showrooms and I bought one of them for cash.

Now in my letter to your company I explained that I owned a 36,000 acre banana and lumber plantation here on the East Coast of Honduras and that up until now I had had the best results with your refrigerator and I gave it all the praise I think is due it. I also explained that because the rubber gasket had rotted out and the seal was not good that it was constantly defrosting and does not in any way give the good service that it had before and would they be kind enough to send me, via air express, a new gasket.

Actually, the warranty that was given to me when I purchased the box should cover this item, but being in the predicament of living away down here in an out-of-the-way place in the tropics, I thought I was being sensible not to press the fact and I felt that the refrigerator was so essential to my living here that I would just as soon pay for the blamed gasket.

In my letter—and please let me digress here for a moment, sir,—I particularly asked the receiver NOT to refer me to their foreign office, or to their foreign representative here in Honduras because I knew from many long years of experience that these agents here will put me off and off again, in the typical mañana fashion and the customer who should deserve some consideration, will toast his heels here in the heat, just waiting . . . waiting . . . waiting . . . until some _____ makes up his mind what to do and when to do it.

Now everything has progressed exactly as I predicted. The recipient of my letter to your factory in July ignored my request—he ignored me, the big sap who shelled out several hundred dollars to buy his company's product. Then he sent my letter on to some joker in your International Division, New York. That probably took a week, while meat spoiled in my refrigerator. The guy who sent that letter to New York should be hunting for another job. Then the guy in the Big Apple, probably after a hilarious week-end at some of the city's discoteques where he had all the ice in the world for his highballs, enters his Pine Street office with bloodshot eyes, passing a half dozen hard working stenographers and secretaries, grunting at each of them as he goes to his plush office, and immediately fixes himself a nice, tall, cool pick-me up and with ice from his refrigerator, and starts the day.

In the interim, I am getting madder and madder, and drinking warm beer, English Highballs without ice, and swearing that I'll never buy another one of your products as long as I live. The warm beer and rum is causing me to think up all sorts of devilish schemes to discourage other planters from ever buying anything you make. How much money do you pay that International Division hot shot to make customers madder than all hell?? I'd fire him too.

The enclosed letter arrived sometime around the middle of August. I bite my tongue and swallow my pride and write to the Horter Company. I know exactly what kind of a reply I am going to receive. I know that old man Horter is an American, a rather seedy old one at that, with an organization of half-breeds, who again are all mañana boys. They are, after a while, going to write me a letter, asking what the serial number of the box is, and the model, and so on and so forth. Then they are going to check up on their previous sales and they are going to discover that they have no record of Cabinet S803A or unit US 803A, so they will then write a nice long letter, asking me where I bought the box, because they have no record of ever having imported it into Honduras.

Of course they have no record of ever having imported it. I smuggled it in on my own banana boat. My father's people were well known smugglers in Ireland hundreds of years ago. My mother's people were Canadian smugglers, between Canada and the State of Michigan. Although I never was a bootlegger, all during prohibition I did smuggle my own rum into Florida from my farm here, and my other property in the Bahamas. It is an honorable hobby.

Sure enough, the Horter Company, on August 23, writes me a letter asking for serial number, model numbers, etc., etc., etc. Damn it all, an 8-foot kerosene Refrigerator is an 8-foot kerosene Refrigerator, and a rubber door gasket is a rubber door gasket.

Now . . . can you do me a great favor? Will you get some sweet little girl in your office to sneak out into the stock room and try to avoid any of the important men who hold down big jobs, and that you undoubtedly overpay for being held down, and have her (when no boss man is looking) steal one (1) rubber gasket for an 8-foot Kerosene Model. Then maybe you and she can, without anybody catching you, wrap it in a piece of paper and airmail it to me. I am an architect—an ex-Army Engineer, and I built dozens of hotels and staff houses from Miami to Africa during the last war, so I think I can possibly put this rubber band on my door without too much difficulty.

I am enclosing a hunk of ticket that came with the box so that no possible slip up can happen. If you can do this for me, without telling any of those blankety-blank young underlings up there about it, maybe some day when you steam into my harbor, I can feed you upon bananas, coconuts, pineapple, and a flock of good tall Methusalem Rum Highballs, made with sparkling ICE CUBES from my now unhappy refrigerator.

Very Sincerely Yours,

J.M._____ P _____

That is a letter. The reply was written by the Chairman of the Board.

The letter reflects his genuine appreciation of the humor in the original—contains a good measure of similar humor—and it pulls no punches. Without going into a detailed rebuttal of the writer's attacks on his company and its officials, he puts the whole affair in proper focus.

Dear Mr. P_____,

    Two sets of rubber gaskets for your eight-foot kerosene refrigerator should reach you by air express about the time you receive this letter. These are sent to you without charge and with my compliments.

    I am taking this action because I got a kick and several good belly laughs out of your letter.

    Smuggling and trafficking with bootleggers may be amusing hobbies, but the price to be paid, as you well know, is getting your tail in the crack occasionally. Then you squawk your head off and attempt to unload your inconvenience and wrath upon the conformists who follow the rules of the game and can't bail you out of trouble because you have fouled the deal.

    The original gasket should not have required replacement unless one of your own crew messed it up with oil. Keep the new gaskets clean, and the refrigerator should be rendering satisfactory service long after you are well under ground.

                Sincerely yours,

Handling a complaint with humor. You are skating on the thinnest of thin ice when you handle a complaint and get funny in your reply. There are times, however, when a skillful letter-writer, detecting evidences of the light touch in the original complaint, can tackle the matter masterfully and bravely with a smile. This is particularly helpful when you are faced with a situation to which there is no fully satisfying reply or remedy.

Exxon Company, U.S.A. – Marine Department received the following letter:

Dear Mr. _____,

    For a long time I have had high regard for anything that is Exxon. Most of the job you do is well done, but as with another great corporation with whom I have a key responsibility—and a good corporate friend of yours—there are frailties, the correction of which very often is merely a matter of attention calling. Regretfully, but indignantly, your correspondent is calling.

Across the way from my home on Riverside Drive, near Edgewater Beach, courting Exxon tankers drop in to pay their respects, leaving the great gallonage of their affectionate regards.

It is quite all right with me and I raise no eyebrows that they drop in at strange hours of the night and tender hours of the morning, but it burns me, lying in bed between the hours of twelve midnight and the dawning hours, to hear them blasting for long periods of time in their bass baritone throats.

No sleep is ever assured for residents on the New York side of the river. We have suffered much too long with the stenches that are Jersey born. Now with increasing disregard for our rest, the tankers raise their voices. Sometimes there is a duet between a tug and a tanker, and not a brief one either. They answer each other with identical signals and occasionally, as on the morning of New Year's Day, from 1:25 until long after 3:00, we are mistreated to a dialog of Wagnerian length.

From all of which, my dear Mr. ＿＿＿＿＿＿＿＿, you will gather I don't think it's nice. I don't think you would either.

Most sincerely yours,

The letter lodges a serious complaint but the writer displayed a sense of humor and a degree of understanding and tolerance. In replying to this mildly worded lament, the writer for Exxon Company made full use of his recognition of these qualities.

Dear Mr. ＿＿＿＿＿＿＿＿,

Your letter of January 5, protesting politely about your inability to sleep through the tooting of tugs and tankers, has been referred to our whistle warblers . . . and you can be sure is having our attention. My occasional absences from the city recently have delayed replying to your letter. To start with, I should like to explain what causes these noises, hoping that, as the French put it, "Tout comprendre, c'est tout pardonner." (If you understand the touts you will pardon the toots.)

A tanker is a big ship, and some of those docks at Edgewater are tough to make, especially when the currents are tricky. It takes two tugs to push the tankers safely into their berths. The docking pilot, who runs the show, stands on the tanker's bridge and handles the tugs from there. Since they are too far away for him to shout, and too close for radio, he toots orders at them.

He uses a police whistle to toot orders to the forward tug, and the tug captain acknowledges by repeating the order with his tug whistle. He toots orders to the after tug with the ship's whistle, and the after tug acknowledges with the tug's whistle.

This isn't something we dreamed up just to be fancier than everybody else. Pilots and masters and tugboat skippers all over the world use a similar system.

The tanker that bothered you on January 1 was the QUEMADO LAKE, which reported tied up at 2:50 A.M. It is not always possible for tankers to arrive in the daytime. It started alongside the dock just as the tide began to ebb, and had a little more trouble than usual, which called for some extra whistle blowing. We imagine the noise, echoing across cliffs, and with the wind blowing the way it was that morning, may well have made you wish you'd never gone to bed at all.

Our Port Captain, who has charge of such things as whistles, will pass the word along to the pilots and tugboat skippers to use no unnecessary toots from now on. Of course, they will have to use some. You no doubt are aware that the Rules of the Road require long blasts now and then. I'm afraid the pilots will have to use the whistles when working the tugs, too—but positively no longer or louder than they absolutely have to.

And surely you will not object to a little toot every now and then. Personally, we think it is a reassuring sound. When all the noise stops, and the harbor goes dead—completely dead—that will be the time to get up and get out. Until then—with thanks for nudging this matter our way—we wish you sound slumber and pleasant dreams.

> Very truly yours,
>
> Exxon Company, U.S.A.
> Marine Department

The humor, you will agree, is light and tactful. Humor is there, but never directed at the reader. Most important, however, is the clear evidence that, despite the jovial tone of the letter, the complaint had been taken very seriously. The reader learns that an investigation has been made. Evidence that this was done—not just said—is introduced when the name of the offending New Year's Eve Tooter, and full details of the specific episode, are included in the letter. Further, it is shown that steps have been taken to reduce the cause of irritation.

The writer made excellent use of well chosen humor but did not try to let humor take the place of service. The combination is ideal.

Collecting with a smile. Seldom is there anything amusing about a past due debt. The company that hasn't been paid isn't laughing and the individual, or company, unwilling or unable to pay, is not likely to find the situation funny. But to all rules there are exceptions. As far as we know the following letter was used just once, but, the author assures us, it worked:

Dear Mr. _____,

I have done more for you than your mother did. Our auditors have pointed out to me that I have carried you for 11 months!

Please deliver.

Sincerely,

POINTS TO BEAR IN MIND WHEN USING HUMOR IN YOUR LETTERS

1. Use humor where you can. It makes people like and trust you.

2. Use appropriate humor, never drag it in just for the sake of saying something funny.

3. Avoid humor if there is any chance that it will irritate.

4. Never use off-color, religious, or political humor.

5. Never make the reader the butt of your humor.

6. Respond to letters written in the light vein, letters that smile and chuckle in the same manner.

7. Answer complaints with a light touch, provided that you are giving a very full answer to the complaint and you feel certain that the complaint isn't so serious to the writer that your humor will be resented.

8. Use humor to attract attention to your reply if you can be certain that it will be an attraction, not a detraction.

17

UNNECESSARY
LETTERS
ARE NECESSARY

The vast majority of the business letters you write must be written. They are intended to accomplish specific tasks, they are responses to letters you have received. Because they are necessary, they are expected. There is no way an expected letter can have the power of unexpected, absolutely unnecessary letters. Those are the letters people will not forget.

After a failed sales presentation. Put yourself in the position created by a personable, intelligent salesperson. You had agreed to the appointment. It was evident that a good deal of preparation time had been invested in the presentation. The inteview was a fairly long one. In the end, however, you decided that you would refuse, and you did.

Nothing unusual about that. It is an everyday business occurrence. Salespeople take their chances. Some they win. Some they lose.

And then, on the following day, you get a thank you letter from the salesperson you turned down. Yes, a thank you letter. Unusual? Not only is it unusual, it is almost unheard of.

Dear Mr. Nodeal,

Thank you, Mr. Nodeal. Of course I would have liked to have come away from your office yesterday with an order. But I'm obeying the impulse to thank you because I did not come away empty-handed.

You gave me a generous amount of your valuable time. You gave me interest and courtesy. You gave me the feeling, Mr. Nodeal, that I had made a new friend.

Gratefully,

Jane Nosale

The salesperson was an able, pleasant person. The chances are that even if the letter had not been written, were you to be asked for another appointment at some time in the future, you might remember her and be willing to see her again. But the letter was written. You will never forget that salesperson for she has done something so exceptional, so extraordinarily pleasant, that she has made an indelible impression on you. Not only will you welcome her back, but you will do so hoping that you will find reason to buy. She is a salesperson you will talk about. If a friend in another company, or another division of your company, happens to mention that they are in the market for something your thank-you-letter salesperson sells, you almost surely will suggest that they call her in.

All of those plusses because an unnecessary letter was written.

Jane Nosale's letter didn't even suggest the possibility of future meetings. All she did was create a thick, lasting layer of good will.

Here is another thank you letter following a refusal:

Dear Mrs. Hamer,

You were right to turn down my suggestion yesterday.

When I came to see you I thought that I was bringing you an appropriate offer, that it represented economy and efficiency for you. The clear and knowledgable way you isolated the negative elements, from your institution's viewpoint, left no room for doubt. You were right.

I appreciate the considerate and friendly manner in which you clarified the uniqueness of your circumstances. My sincere hope is that I'll have the opportunity to call on you again one day—this time with a concept that has substantial benefits for you.

Cordially,

Joe Nosale

In this letter Joe not only thanked his refuser, he actually agreed with her decision. He flattered her *for not buying*. At the same time he let her know that he was not crossing her off of his list of prospects. He made it clear that what he had learned from her would be applied to his next effort to make a sale. That puts even more oil on the hinges of the open office door.

This has been a bad season for Joe, for here he is, with still one more needless letter:

Dear Mr. Maker,

That was an exceptionally interesting, stimulating meeting I had at your plant yesterday. Thanks for making it so instructive.

You gave me a great deal to think about.

When I returned to my offices I told our president of your very valid reasons for not accepting our proposal. He agreed with you. You have no substantial basis for believing that our system will give you the economies I projected. His conclusion, I'm particularly pleased to say, is that we should prove the potential benefits at our own expense. That can be done if you will permit one of our senior engineers to spend several days in your production area, observing, making time and motion studies, and then preparing a detailed analysis and comparison for your review.

I will phone you Thursday morning to ask when I may bring Mr. Pilot, the engineer, to your offices to meet you. He will describe, in detail, what he may be able to accomplish for you.

Cordially,

Joe Nosale

Joe and Jane habitually write unnecessary letters whenever they get turned down, but the composition of each one requires creative thought. In the course of preparing the letter to Mr. Maker, he saw a way to use the reasons for refusal to pave the way to reconsideration. This letter thus had the benefits of the pleasantly unexpected and a most acceptable counter to Mr. Maker's basis for the turn down.

Underlying much of the value of the thank you letter after a no sale presentation are the emotional needs of the recipient. Nobody, and this includes hard boiled professional buyers, enjoys saying no to decent, pleasant, well informed, and businesslike sales people. When you are in a buying situation you know that it inflates your ego, makes you feel good, when you say yes. In sharp contrast, when it is necessary to refuse you feel ill at ease, uncomfortable. Anything the salesperson does to ease your discomfort you appreciate. An unnecessary thank you letter received the day after the failed presentation not only eases your feelings of guilt, you are grateful to the salesperson for the broad-minded appreciation of the elements that led to the refusal. You have been conditioned to welcome a future opportunity to do business with someone who has shown you so much consideration.

Tribute to loyal customers. Joe and Jane Nosale aren't the only ones who can use unnecessary letters to great advantage. Consider the impact of this one:

Dear Charlotte,

This morning I saw several letters being prepared welcoming and
thanking new customers. That goes on every working day. It suddenly
struck me that this is nonsense.

I don't mean that it is nonsense to thank a new customer, but it is
nonsense that I have never taken the time to drop a line to you to tell you
how deeply I appreciate your consistent loyalty. You have been a
splendid customer for years . . . splendid in terms of being so
wonderfully pleasant to deal with, not just because of the volume of your
purchases.

Please accept a warm and sincerely felt thank you for being you and
for all of the business you have sent our way.

Cordially,

Ruth

Charlotte has no reason to question the genuineness of the senti-
ments expressed in that letter. She knows that she has been a very loyal
customer of Ruth's company, that the relationship has always been a
pleasant one. She also knows that she is equally loyal to various other
resources, but the chances are great that she never has had a letter like
this from any of them. Ruth becomes, and will remain, a standout in
her mind. At times when business falls off, or when some misunderstanding between Charlotte and Ruth's company happens to occur,
that simple little needless letter can put a great deal of weight on Ruth's
side of the scale.

Do you handle credit?

Dear Mr. Payer,

As credit manager I have a whole series of letters we use when people
fall behind in their payments.

Today, when your check for your recent purchase crossed my desk, I
suddenly realized that there is far greater reason to write a letter to
you—to create a new kind of letter.
And this is it . . .

Thank you, Mr. Payer,
For as long as you have been dealing with us you invariably have
met your obligations on time or ahead of time. You merit
recognition far more than those who are indifferent or careless about
such matters. Were it not for you, and the other solid, conscientious

people we serve, profits would be lower and prices would be higher.
Life would be far less enjoyable.

You are appreciated,

Mr. George Cash

Mr. Payer is probably going to give that rare letter a lot of
circulation. He will carry it with him and display it to as many people
as he can, always of course, to point out what fine people George
Cash's company employ. It is low cost, high value advertising that
cannot help but be productive. And it is a fairly safe assumption that
should Mr. Payer ever experience financial difficulties, George Cash
will be the last of his creditors to detect any sign of it.

Appreciation of civic spirit. Then there are needless unnecessary
letters. All of those you have read up to this point have very clear
motives. The writer hopes to convert a nonbuyer to a buyer eventually,
aims to make a good customer even better, seeks to weld a top credit
customer more firmly to the buying habit he has established.
But consider this one:

Dear Mrs. Chamer,

Without ever having had the pleasure of meeting you I feel that I know
you. Frequently I see items in the paper related to your selfless activities
for the good of our community and for our less fortunate neighbors.
I just had to obey the impulse to express my admiration and gratitude.

Sincerely,

Mark Green

Mark Green may be in the real estate business, securities, insurance,
or he may be owner or an executive of some retail store. It doesn't
matter. The great beauty of the letter, beyond its being totally
unnecessary and unexpected, is that it asks for nothing, suggests
nothing, invites nothing in return. It simply expresses one person's
appreciation of the activities of a civic-minded individual. If you
participate in charity, church, or any other types of community work,
you know how exceptional such recognition is. You know, too, that
Mrs. Chamer is bound to be delighted to receive such a letter. You can
picture the degree to which she will share it with fellow workers, her
family, and her friends. Mark Green didn't ask for any business but the
likelihood that letters of that type will bring him new clients is almost
certain.

Salespeople who travel, have some special problems and v
appear to be unnecessary letters can be extremely effective to
which to deal with some of them. Tom Dooray covers three sta
of his problems is that he cannot see even his most active customers as
frequently as he would like. He knows that Paul Blue, for instance,
often runs low on some of the items he buys from Tom and is inclined
to restock by buying from whoever happens to call on him when he
sees his inventory getting low. Tom found the solution with this letter:

Dear Paul,

I always enjoy calling on you and wish my territory permitted me to
come by more often. The fact that I can't come by as often as I would
like has worried me. There are times, I know, when I could be useful.

Please make a note of my home phone number, Paul—(212)
768-8797. While on the road I contact the office once a week, but I call
my wife almost every day. If there is ever anything I can do for you
please place a collect call. Grace will relay your message to me and I'll
be on top of anything you need or want in a hurry.

My best to you . . .

Tom

The letter indirectly asks for business but in a way that reflects
genuine concern for, and interest in, Paul's convenience. Tom has
made it easier for his customer to order from him than to wait for the
next competitive salesman to show up. It is a warm, inviting, and
practical letter.

The one other time Tom Dooray is absent from the selling scene is
while on vacation. Believing in the adage, "out of sight, out of mind,"
he employs unnecessary postcards to let each of his customers know
why he is not making his customary calls, but in a manner that
increases the good will he customarily works to build.

Dear Mr. Leith,

This is one of the most enjoyable vacations I've had in years. While
exercising the proverbial fisherman's patience this afternoon I did a bit of
day-dreaming-philosophizing. Being in an unusually happy mood I got to
thinking of all the people who contribute so much to my enjoyment of
life. You were high on the list and I just thought I'd pass the thought
along. See you next month.

Tom

Actually, Tom didn't disrupt his vacation by sitting in a hotel room writing postcards to all of his customers. Around the time he made his reservation, he sought and received the cooperation of the hotel. He had them send him the number of postcards he needed. He wrote, addressed, and stamped all of them during leisure hours well before his vacation. He packed them with his hip boots and fishing gear, and mailed them when he arrived on the scene.

A customer writes an unnecessary letter. A good friend of mine told me of this experience. She and her husband had sold their home and bought a condominium unit in an apartment house. Originally, they had been told that they could not actually make the move until mid-November. One day in September, however, they got a phone call. The former occupants had moved out and they could make their move whenever they pleased.

This delighted them since the people who had bought their house were pressing them. One problem. They wanted their carpets picked up, cut, and laid before having the furniture moved. Friends in a similar situation had warned them that most carpet people had long waiting lists.

Mrs. B_____ phoned the carpet company. She asked for the owner and got him on the phone. After introducing herself she said that seven years before she had called on them to recarpet her home; that they had done such fine work she was looking forward to working with them again and was faced with a time problem. Before she could go any further the man she was talking to interrupted her. He said, "Yes, Mrs. B_____, you now live at Brandywine and 31st Street, right?"

She was astonished. "What an amazing memory you have," she exclaimed. "No," he replied, "you wrote us a letter the last time we served you and I have it in a frame on my desk, right in front of me. How soon do you want us to go to work?"

This was the letter:

President

Newtown Floor Coverings

Your installers have just finished laying wall-to-wall carpeting throughout the first floor of our home. They did a beautiful job, they were courteous and considerate and I particularly appreciated the thorough clean-up they did when the work was done.

I thought you would enjoy knowing how well your people represent you.

Sincerely,

Mrs. Fred B_____

If he had framed her letter and had it on his desk, how many letters of that type do you suppose he has received? Hers was a never-happened-before expression of gratitude for work well done. Her reward was not a great one, but a reward all the same. Have you ever written to any of your business resources to just express deserved admiration of the way they serve you? Can you visualize the impact that such letters might have in time of shortages, when emergency measures are needed, when you might want to request an extension of credit, when you would like them to accept the return of some goods?

Unnecessary letters constitute a fine form of selfish selflessness. The question is, are unnecessary letters really necessary?

THINGS TO KEEP IN MIND WHEN WRITING UNNECESSARY LETTERS

1. Thanking someone who refused your offer marks you as an outstanding and unusual individual.

2. Your letter after a refusal can suggest future efforts.

3. When composing a thank-you letter following a refusal, consider what might be said to invite reconsideration.

4. How many good, long-term customers do you have who merit, but have never received, special letters of appreciation?

5. Have you ever expressed your admiration of people or companies who consistently meet their obligation on time or earlier?

6. Scan the social pages of your papers to see who you might sincerely thank for consistent volunteer work that benefits your community.

7. As a travelling salesperson, what customer problems might you make lighter with a between-calls letter?

8. A friendly letter or card while on vacation flatters the recipients and increases your own stature.

18

LEARNING
TO HANDLE
DELICATE SITUATIONS

You've now read 17 chapters on how to write letters. You've read some of the fine effective business letters being used with success, by lots of well known companies.

The things you have read have given you a variety of attitude direction-finders and some practical points. These can serve to make your own letters warm, complete, and compelling. They have covered the routine letters that come across your desk, the standard inquiries that must be answered, letters you originate.

This chapter is your postgraduate course.

In this chapter, let's take a look at the problem of writing responses that are *really* tough.

And because this is a postgraduate course, suppose you see how much you've learned, how well you are doing. Here are six letter-writing problems. Read the problems. Study them carefully. Think about them. Adjust your mental attitude and then write the letters of reply.

After you have written your letters—not before—turn to the sample replies on the pages that follow. Read the letters and the analysis of each and measure *your* letters against the samples. See if you are satisfied that you have thought of every point. Tell yourself whether or not your letters were as strong and as effective as they might have been.

PROBLEM NO. 1—WRONG NUMBER

You are in the mail order business. Twice a year you produce a catalog of household and gift items. You mail the catalog to old and prospective customers. A good customer has just received your Christmas catalog. She is a business executive who has been selecting her firm's Christmas gifts from your catalogs for a number of years.

You get a letter from her ordering 100 desk clocks. But she has made an error. The clock she has specified is not in your catalog. It is featured in a competitor's catalog. You have a similar clock. Your clock sells for $26.00 a unit. The competitor's clock is $24.50.

Your agreement with the manufacturer of the clock you handle does not permit you to lower the price. The only advantage your clock has over the competitive brand is that your clock has a radium dial and swivels on its base, while the other has a plain dial and is in a fixed position. Write to your customer.

PROBLEM NO. 2—WHERE, OH WHERE?

You work for a manufacturing plant. This letter comes to your attention.

Gentlemen:

More than three weeks ago I saw your ad in the PDQ Trade Journal. I wrote to you, in response to the ad enclosing my check for $142.78, a copy of the ad, and a covering letter, ordering one gross of your Model 0021, to be shipped to me Express collect.

I have not received the merchandise. You haven't even had the courtesy to acknowledge my order. If you are not prepared to ship the ordered merchandise, immediately return my check.

Sincerely,

O.P. Hattery

PROBLEM NO. 3—STUDENT TROUBLE

You conduct a correspondence school in typewriter cleaning and repair work. Students make a down payment of $50 and then pay $20 a month for 16 months while taking the course.

Joe Typer has been taking the course for seven months. His assignments and payments have come in promptly. His work has been excellent. Now you get a letter from him instead of his completed assignment:

Dear Gentlemen,

I have bad news. The whole time I've been taking your course I've been working and doing the lessons at night. My wife has been working too. Now she's broken her leg. The right one.

Now I have to work at night too. I fix the dinner. I wash the dishes. I do the laundry. I clean the apartment. I help the kids with their homework and put them to bed and I have to tend to my wife too. I'm too tired to do anything else. I quit.

Yours very truly,

Joe Typer

When Joe started the course he signed a binding contract. He is legally liable for the balance of the payments whether he completes the course or not. This is your own school. What you say to him is up to you. Write to Joe Typer.

PROBLEM NO. 4—THE CANTANKEROUS LANDLORD

The insurance agency you head occupies half a floor of a large but old office building. You have been in the building for twelve years. Two years ago the building was sold. Mrs. Clay, the new owner, resides in a distant city. You have never met her. She has refused to renew leases for any of the building's occupants. You are on a month-to-month basis. This morning you had a letter from the owner. She tells you she has decided to completely modernize the building. In order to do so in the least expensive and most efficient manner, she is giving all tenants 30 days notice to move.

Office space is difficult to obtain and you are in the midst of your busiest season. Write a letter to the owner.

PROBLEM NO. 5—OUT OF CASH

You are Harry Elect. You own and operate a retail outlet for electric appliances. Business has been fairly slack, but you count on good volume during the Christmas season. You stock heavily. Business is good, but not as good as you had hoped. Right after Christmas some new merchandise of various types comes on the market. Heavy national advertising by the manufacturers builds up a healthy demand.

You order the new merchandise in. You know you have to do some local advertising to let people know what you have. The combination of these conditions puts you in bad shape for current finances. Your bank has loaned you as much money as they will. Your resources are beginning to press you for payment.

A letter arrives from the sales manager of your biggest supplier. She tells you she is unable to ship the goods you just ordered because her credit department advises her that you are behind in your payment for previous shipments. Your greatest hopes were based on your offering of her goods. Your advertising, already being printed, features that merchandise. There is nothing you can do about sending her company a check now. Write to her.

PROBLEM NO. 6–GET RICH QUICK

You are an investment dealer. Mr. Bowers, an elderly widower, is one of your clients. He has sufficient capital to produce the income he needs, provided that he lives carefully and that none of his capital is used for luxurious living expenses, or exposed to needless risks. You have taken great pains to invest his money in highly conservative securities that give him the income his situation requires.

Today you get a letter from Mr. Bowers. He is visiting friends in a distant city. He tells you that he met a salesperson for an investment firm there. On his advice, he wants to sell a number of his current securities and use that money to buy stock of the CDQ Mining and Exploration Company. The man he met has assured him that he can double his money within six months.

You look up the CDQ stock and you see that it pays no dividends at all, that the value of the securities is highly questionable; that Mr. Bowers is more likely to lose his money than double it. Write to him.

Have you written your letters of reply? Go over them carefully. Edit them. Picture yourself talking on the telephone, using the words you've written. Do they sound right? Are they warm? Do they take the other party's viewpoint into consideration? Do they cover all essential points? Does each one start with a statement that will lure the reader into wanting to know what comes next? Does each start with a tone that will set the stage for the reader to feel well disposed toward you? Has each letter an ending that pinpoints the action you want and that makes it as easy as possible for the reader to take action?

Are your thoughts presented in logical order? Have you sidestepped the use of tired, worn-out expressions? Are your words and sentences simple and clear? Does each letter flow smoothly, avoiding abrupt, puzzling shifts of thought?

Does each letter show that you formed a sharp mental picture of the person you've written to? Where you had to refuse a request, did you show that great consideration had been given to the proposition, before you turned it down. Did you start and end your letters of refusal with something the reader would enjoy reading?

If you are satisfied that your letters are as good as they should be, read the sample answers. Compare them with your own letters. See if the analysis of each sample letter could apply to *your* own efforts.

REPLY TO PROBLEM NO. 1—WRONG NUMBER

Dear Ms. Obermann,

Although thousands of orders come in at this time of the year, the ones that get the warmest greetings are those from loyal customers, like you. You've given us your Christmas order for many years. Every transaction we've had with you has been exceptionally pleasant.

Undoubtedly, at this time of the year you are snowed under with catalogs from many mail order houses. It would be nice to think that our catalog was the only one that claimed your attention, but of course that isn't so, nor would it be good business on your part. Evidently, you read at least one other catalog this year. The Desk Clocks you specified are not carried by us.

I've done some checking for you. The clock you ordered is offered by Joe Stow & Co., 212 98th Street in Keokok, Iowa. If you feel that the Stow clocks will serve your purposes best, that's where they are.

But, Ms. Obermann, I hope you will take another look at the Desk Clocks on page 131 of our catalog. You'll be particularly interested in Model 41. Model 41 is almost identical to the clock you selected, with two exceptions. Our clock has a radium dial and swivel base, giving your customers added convenience. The prices of the two clocks are almost the same. The two additional values in Model 41 add only $1.50 a unit to your cost. In case your copy of the catalog has been discarded, I'm enclosing another one for you.

Desk Clocks seem to be unusually popular this year and Model 41 has been selling immensely well. To be certain that your needs will be covered, I'm putting aside the 100 you want. I'll hold them until I hear from you.

After you've read this letter, please phone me collect to tell me whether you want the folks on your Christmas list to have Model 41. Your clocks are sitting on the shipping room "hold" counter, all prettied up in their sparkling Christmas wrappings. They're ready to go to you the moment you say, "Okay." I'll be grateful if you'll give me your decision by Friday of this week.

Sincerely,

Analysis

Setting the atmosphere. The opening paragraph performs several useful functions. In a warm, friendly manner, the first sentence reminds Ms. Obermann of the order she placed. The balance of the paragraph creates the mental atmosphere needed under the circumstances. She's reminded of her "loyalty," of the fact that she's given this firm her Christmas orders each year and that all transactions have been "exceptionally pleasant." The desirability of dealing with this mail order house has been implanted in her mind firmly and with flattering courtesy.

Stating the situation. The second paragraph tells of the error that was made. Great tact has been used to avoid the possibility of Ms. Obermann feeling foolish and ill at ease. She is even complimented on her good business judgment in looking at competitive catalogs.

Extreme service. In the third paragraph, the writer caters fully to Ms. Obermann's interests. Although he wants the business the writer spells out the fact that he went to the trouble to learn where Ms. Obermann can get the competitive item if she wants it above all others. This is extreme service and consideration. It cannot fail to make a deep impression on Ms. Obermann. The writer is so immensely fair and helpful that the desire to do business with him soars to new heights. What he has done is so unusual the act will be remembered for years to come. Ms. Obermann can become a great spreader of good will for the company.

Making the sale. The fourth paragraph makes a strong and logical bid for the order. Without deprecating the competitive article, the writer builds up the greater desirability of his own. He makes it completely easy for the buyer to examine it by telling her precisely where to find the illustration and description in the catalog. To be sure that no chance is lost, he even encloses a duplicate copy of the catalog. In telling of the higher price, he presents it in the most desirable manner. First he tells what the extra qualities are and then he quotes the price in the lowest denominator. He speaks of $1.50 a unit not $26.00 a unit.

Prelude to action. The fifth paragraph starts the drive for the desired action. Without seeming to put undue pressure on Ms. Obermann, the need for fast action is made clear. Model 41 is going fast. Fine service to Ms. Obermann is clear again. Because Model 41 is going fast, the writer protects his customer's interest by holding the needed quantity for her.

Action. Now, in the final paragraph, the wanted action is detailed. It is made cost-free and simple. An additional advantage is piled on. Ms. Obermann is given a mental picture of the attractive Christmas wrappings. Speed of delivery is held before her as still another benefit. The letter ends by requesting action by a specific date.

REPLY TO PROBLEM NO. 2—WHERE, OH WHERE?

Dear Mr. Hattery,

One gross of Model 0021 left here by Air Express this morning, twenty minutes after your letter arrived. By this time, you've had my telegram advising you of the shipment.

My warmest thanks, Mr. Hattery, for writing and bringing this inexcusable delay to the surface. You've been very patient.

The moment your shipment was out of here and the telegram sent, I started an investigation. Until you've had some more experience with us, you'll find it hard to believe, I'm sure, but this is far from our normal method of handling orders.

The rule here is that an order is acknowledged the day it arrives and, if humanly possible, the goods are shipped that same day. The longest we normally take to make a shipment is 48 hours, unless we have no inventory of the item requested. That's why your well justified complaint constituted a serious mystery here.

I didn't have to look far. The first place checked was the accounting department. Your order and check went there first to be entered on the books and to permit them to search the files to see if you were a new customer or not. They found that you had placed one previous order nearly three years ago. And that's where it happened. When the old folder was returned to the file your new order went in the file too. That's where it was found this morning.

No heads rolled. Nobody was fired. The folks working in that department are good. They handle thousands of details each week and they make amazingly few errors. But they are human and mistakes will happen. We had a little meeting and showed them what had occurred in your case. It put everyone that much more on their toes to safeguard against a similar slip in the future.

So, we owe you more than a deeply sincere apology, Mr. Hattery. We owe you a vote of genuine appreciation. The incident will make us even more efficient in the future.

I do hope that the delay didn't cause you any serious inconvenience.

Please accept our warmest thanks for your business. I look forward to hearing from you again so that we'll be able to demonstrate the far more normal courtesy and speed with which your orders will be handled. Although your letter specified that the merchandise should be sent express collect we have prepaid the shipment, to demonstrate our desire to make amends.

Sincerely,

Analysis

Tell your reader the action taken at once. Mr. Hattery's greatest interest is to find out what you're going to do. The opening paragraph, therefore, gives him that information without frills or prelude.

Unruffle a reader's feathers. With good cause, the customer was upset. The second paragraph pours some oil on the troubled waters and the following paragraph adds to the desired effect. It lets Mr. Hattery know that his letter caused deep concern and instant investigation. That's flattering.

Full explanation. The next item of importance is to establish the fact that this type of handling is highly unusual in your plant. A full explanation is essential. The fourth and fifth paragraphs tell the story. The story is complete and it is believable.

This isn't normal here. The explanation may tell how it happened, but you have another important job to perform. You have to convince the customer that, despite his experience, you have an efficient organization. Paragraph six tackles that job, and number seven ties the bow on the package.

Something extra. The final paragraph makes a bid for future business and gives the customer a bonus to make amends for the discourtesy and the delay. It is bound to leave Mr. Hattery thinking, "Aren't they nice people!"

REPLY TO PROBLEM NO. 3 – STUDENT TROUBLE

Dear Mr. Typer,

I don't blame you a bit. If I had the problems that are sitting on your shoulders right now, chances are I would have written the same letter you just wrote to me.

Of course you can't find time to carry on your home assignments, and give them the concentration they deserve, with all those troubles and duties at home. I wouldn't expect or want you to.

You've been doing a fine job up to this point. Seven months ago you saw an opportunity to do something that would lead you to a real career. You made your decision and went to work. You've worked well—unusually well—and the realization of your ambition is not far off. Now there's been a disruption. But this present condition won't last forever, Mr. Typer. You'll still reach your goal.

I'm putting your papers in a special file on my desk. On top of it I've written, "Hold in suspense for three months." That means that you won't have to do any assignments or make another payment for three months. You're being given a leave of absence until your home situation is back where it was before your wife's unfortunate accident.

All of us here hope that Mrs. Typer makes a quick and painless recovery. The only thing I'm going to ask you to do right now is to return the postcard I'm putting in with this letter. Three months is my guess as to the length of time you'll need. If you think the time should be shorter or longer, or if you agree with my guess, just tell me on the card and drop it in the mail. That way I'll know when to send along your next lesson.

Good luck and thanks for letting me know the circumstances.

Cordially,

Analysis

You're right! Joe Typer's letter makes it clear that he's disturbed and unhappy. He's in a state of rebellion. He has told you that he's quitting. Undoubtedly he expects you to write back telling him he can't or shouldn't quit. He's mentally prepared for that, and he's prepared to resist you. The opening paragraphs of this letter take the wind out of his sails. The School agrees with him. He's told he's right, that he's doing what anybody would do. Joe's mental resistance to the expected onslaught evaporates.

Ambition rekindled. Seven months ago Joe Typer had a vision. The vision was strong enough to impel him to put up his hard earned money and devote a lot of his spare time to make that vision a reality. Those are strong motivations. Deep down inside of Joe, a good percentage of that vision and determination must exist today. It's been buried by immediate problems. The writer, recognizing this, uses the third paragraph to trade on these elements. He rekindles the ambition. In doing so he reminds Joe that his work with the course has been unusually good. This is pleasing and it adds reality to the rewards the promised career can provide.

Understanding is good business. While the earlier paragraphs indicate sympathy and understanding, the fourth paragraph puts them on a practical basis. The School's action shows Joe a way out of his troubles without giving up his career ambitions. The offer makes it easy for him to make the decision that he can and will complete the course.

Not a word is said about his contractual obligation to the School. The tone of the letter is that the writer wants to help a friend. You don't talk to a friend about helping him in one breath and then threaten to sue him in the next. You don't even hint at such a possibility. If Joe fails to accept this generous offer, it may become necessary to use pressure in some future letters. In this first one, however, it would be completely out of order.

Ask for action. At a casual glance, it may not seem necessary to ask for any kind of action now. Actually, the need is urgent. If the action request is absent, the chances are that Joe will not respond. The School, under those circumstances, will have to wait for three months before they know whether Joe is going to continue or not. That is bad. The company is in a far better situation if they are told that Joe still wants to quit. They can take immediate action by writing additional letters of encouragement and persuasion. Eventually, if need be, they can become firm and enforce their legal rights.

On the other hand, if Joe returns the requested postcard now, saying that he will start again when his home life returns to normal, he has made a mental and moral commitment. The chances are he'll see it through. The postcard is essential.

REPLY TO PROBLEM NO. 4 – THE CANTANKEROUS LANDLORD

Dear Mrs. Clay,

Sincerest congratulations on the progressive move you are about to make. You have a fine building here. The location is one of the best in the city. Now you plan to make the building as modern and as desirable as any of the new buildings that have grown up around us. It's a splendid plan.

When your letter arrived this morning I cancelled all my engagements for the day. I have phoned or visited nearly a dozen office buildings and real estate offices in an effort to make satisfactory arrangements that would enable me to comply with your request. So far I've found nothing.

The half floor we've been occupying for the past twelve years is a lot of space. Finding an equal amount of space in any office building in town, I've learned, is going to be a real problem. Immediate occupancy is what makes this difficult. In several buildings, there will be adequate space available in three to six months, but not sooner.

What is the best way for me to cooperate with you, Mrs. Clay? As you know, our offices are on the second floor. How long do you think it will be before your workmen reach my part of the building?

At this time, Mrs. Clay, I would like to apply for a long-term lease in your renovated building. Perhaps, if your plans call for the completion of the upper stories first, we can figure out a way I can stay where I am until one of the upper floors is completed and then move right into that part of the building.

I'll phone you Thursday morning at 10:30 to discuss this idea with you.

Cordially,

Analysis

Surprise. Perhaps there are as many as 100 tenants in your building. On the morning you received your letter, identical letters reached everyone else. There's little doubt that, within 48 hours, Mrs. Clay's desk was piled high and her phone burning. Tenant after tenant with red hot answers. They would start out by pouring abuse on her head. Many would drip with tears as the writers told their sad stories. A good percentage would cry out about the long years they had paid their rent month after month—and then to be treated like this!

Out of this heap of bitterness, anger, self-righteousness, and self-pity Mrs. Clay would find few, if any, who looked at the problem from *her* viewpoint.

Paragraph one actually pats her on the back. It recognizes her progressiveness. It makes her feel wise and enterprising. Here's a letter she can read with pleasure and with an open mind.

Cooperation. In the second paragraph, Mrs. Clay gets her second happy surprise. This tenant actually dropped everything and made a real try to comply with the request that he get out in thirty days.

The third paragraph develops this theme further and reveals some of the inescapable problems involved.

The fourth paragraph elaborates on the cooperation theme and sets forth a possible solution to the difficulty. The writer has taken the initiative in suggesting a way out. He has not written saying he can't do it. *He* has done the thinking.

Temptation. Mrs. Clay will have to find tenants for her reconstructed building. Here's an offer to take a half floor. Coupled with the offer, is the suggestion of how Mrs. Clay and the writer can work out a plan that will be mutually beneficial.

Action. The writer spells out what action he will take. He doesn't leave the next step up to the harassed Mrs. Clay, but takes the bit in his own teeth.

In a situation of this type it is quite possible that the cantankerous landlord will not do anything for anybody. It is also possible, however, that her reconstruction plans will permit her to forestall the need for some occupants to move as quickly as others. Abuse and chest-pounding have little chance of winning you whatever dispensation Mrs. Clay can hand out. The sample letter shown here creates an atmosphere that would encourage Mrs. Clay to give you the utmost consideration. It is simply a matter of looking at every problem from the other person's viewpoint.

REPLY TO PROBLEM NO. 5—OUT OF CASH

Dear Joan,

If I were your credit manager I'd do exactly what he or she did. I am behind in my payments right now and that's what he or she has to watch. He's on his toes.

But, Joan, while he watches credits you watch business and you watch the people you sell to. I'm only one of your many customers, but I believe you know how we went all out with your line this Christmas. As an alert sales manager you know, too, that Christmas business was not what any of us expected.

Your Christmas goods—a fair part of them—are still here and I haven't called on you to take any of them off my hands. You have wonderful merchandise and I know we'll sell it, given enough time. And now you've proven again what great merchandisers you are by bringing out your new line and backing it up with equally great national promotion.

The demand is here. Folks are asking for your items and I'm spurring that interest by doing a big local advertising job on your new lines.

If you and I were sitting in your office or mine, right now, and you were the president of your company, I know perfectly well you'd back me up. And I know what a top salesperson you are, Joan. As a personal favor to me, and for the broader distribution of your own goods, Joan I'm asking you to sit down with your credit person and sell him or her Harry Elect.

My business is sound. I need time and I need help to get out from behind my over-heavy inventory, which I will do. My bills will be paid and your house will be the first to know it—with checks—when those consumer dollars come in.

I'll call you Friday morning.

> Cordially,
>
> Harry Elect

Analysis

The writer's right. The normal, immediate reaction to the bad news from your supplier would be indignation, bitterness at past loyalties being forgotten, deep disappointment. But the expression of any of these emotions is not calculated to get you what you need and want. On sober second thought you can, with complete honesty, appreciate the credit problems faced by a big manufacturer. To the credit office you are no more than a ledger card or line or two on a computer printout. Right now what a credit manager reads about you doesn't look too good.

The first paragraph says that you know she's right. You compliment her on her alertness. This gets the letter off to an acceptable, interesting start. It does something more. You are asking the sales manager to go to bat for you with the credit manager. You've put a beautiful tool in her hands. She can show your letter to the credit manager and what you said can only help—cannot hurt—your cause.

Flattery. The second and third paragraphs express sincere appreciation for the sales manager's capabilities and your admiration for the company and its products. The words you've used about the sales manager appeal to her ego and to her business judgment. They make her *want* to understand and appreciate your current problem.

The fourth paragraph lets her know that her company has your full loyalty and support. You are devoting your advertising to the promotion of her merchandise.

Challenge. On the dual basis of helping her company and you, the fifth paragraph goads the sales manager with a friendly challenge to display her sales ability, her knowledge of people, and of markets by going to bat for Harry Elect.

Confidence. Without exaggeration or too much stress, the sixth paragraph builds confidence in the basic soundness of Harry Elect and his store. It promises, too, that payment will not be long in coming.

Action. Taking the action on his own shoulders, Harry Elect accomplishes two vital objectives. He eliminates the need to sit and worry while hoping and waiting for a reply. He also placed the sales manager in a position where she cannot put off doing something about Harry Elect's request, no matter how busy she may be. That phone call is coming on Friday morning and she must have an answer by that time.

REPLY TO PROBLEM NO. 6 – GET RICH QUICK

Dear Mr. Bowers,

Of course you would like to double your money. I understand exactly how you feel. The hope that such a thing will happen for them is what pulls hundreds of thousands of people to the race tracks and to the gambling casinos every day. But there's one great difference between those people and you. When gamblers place a bet on a horse, a card, or a number, they do so with the full realization that the money they put up will bring them no dividends or interest, and, if they happen to be wrong, the money is gone forever.

Mr. Bowers, you and I have had some long sessions together. You have been frank and open with me, trusting me as your counsellor, and I know how important it is to you to preserve every bit of your capital. You've shown me the vital need to keep that money working for you so that it can produce the income you need for your living expenses.

I would be doing you a serious disservice if I did not warn you, as emphatically as I know how, against the step you are considering.

As soon as your letter arrived, I investigated the CDQ Mining and Exploration Company. The reports and statements I read were long, but the information boils down to a few simple facts. At the present time there are no facts available to give you, or anyone else, any sound reason to believe that investors will realize any profits, or that they are protected from serious loss. The future welfare of the Company is based on pure chance. CDQ's past history has not been good and no changes have taken place in management or policy to give promise of any change for the better. They could, of course, get lucky, but, in my opinion, the chances of losing whatever sum you invest is far greater than the chance or relizing a profit.

Your money and your securities, Mr. Bowers, are your property and, of course, you have the liberty to do with them as you will. As your counsellor, and as a friend, I urge you not to go into this proposed venture.

Sincerely,

Analysis

The temptation is understandable . . . but. While this letter starts with a measure of sympathetic understanding, it quickly shifts to a shocking contrast. The writer, knowing Mr. Bowers and his financial circumstances, realizes that he would never consider taking his precious capital and gambling with it at the track or roulette table. The opening of this letter puts him on notice that he is contemplating a move that is equally reckless.

Security . . . not wealth. Mr. Bowers is reminded of his true needs and goals. At his age, he needs security far more than sudden wealth. This portion of the letter reminds him of that basic fact. At the same time it serves to reestablish the shared confidence of the relationship between him and his investment counsellor: an important reminder at this time.

The writer shows that he took the time and trouble to investigate the CDQ Company, for Mr. Bowers' benefit. He strips the situation down to the essential truths so that Mr. Bowers can see, for himself, the great risk he would be taking.

You have a free choice. The final paragraph of the letter puts the power of final decision in Mr. Bower's hands. The writer is not dictating to him. He is giving him counsel and allowing him the face-saving opportunity to say, "I have decided not to take this big risk."

How well did you do? Are you satisfied that the letters you wrote handled each of the six situations as fully and as understandingly as the sample replies?

This exercise is less a test of writing skills than a test of *attitudes*.

Compare the attitudes your letters reflect with the attitudes displayed in the sample letters. *Are you satisfied that the approach you took, in each case, is calculated to lead the reader to take the action you want?* Are your letters stripped of irritants? Has each of the letters taken full recognition of the *reader's point of view?*

If you are *not* satisfied that your own letters did all the things they should do, look for the missing elements, search for the sour notes. See what you *could* have done to make your own letters—your own action requests—as easily acceptable as the samples.

What you are seeking is *not* a way to write these particular letters: *you are looking for the key to a winning attitude in all of the letters you will write from this day on.*

NOW WHERE
DID I SEE THAT LETTER?
INSTANT LOCATOR

A few people—but mighty few—are blessed with photographic memories. They can read a book of 300 or more pages and recall exactly which pages contained specific items they want to review.

Since most of us lack that spectacular skill we lose a lot of time and patience in the digging process. This Instant Locator is designed to help you to find any special letters you want to refer to now, or in the future.

The cross index that follows has 5 divisions:

1. Company Names
2. Points Illustrated
3. Business, Products, or Services
4. Purpose of Letter
5. Quotations

Perhaps the feature that remains uppermost in your mind is an opening statement or a highlighted statement. All opening statements and featured statements that are at all memorable are listed under Quotations.

The distinction between category 2, Points Illustrated, and 4, Purpose of Letter, is that the use of humor may be the point illustrated in a letter whose purpose is to collect a past due account. No matter which aspect of the letter you happen to recall, you can find it with ease. You may remember that what you are looking for is a letter from a printer, but you can't recall the name of the company . . . or vice versa. It doesn't matter. You'll find what you want by going to the category you do remember.

(The "Exercise" letters in Chapter 18 are not included.)

BUSINESS, PRODUCTS, OR SERVICES

PURPOSE OF LETTER

QUOTATIONS

Opening statements